SPIRITUALISM

IDENTICAL WITH

ANCIENT SORCERY, NEW TESTAMENT DEMONOLOGY, AND MODERN WITCHCRAFT:

WITH THE TESTIMONY OF GOD AND MAN AGAINST IT.

BY W. M'DONALD.

New York:
PUBLISHED BY CARLTON & PORTER,
200 MULBERRY-STREET.
1866.

PREFACE.

THE author of this volume was appointed, by the "Providence District Ministers' Association," to prepare an essay on the "History of Spiritualism." Two years subsequent to the appointment the essay was read before the Association, when the following resolution was passed with regard to its publication:

"*Resolved*, That Rev. W. M'Donald be respectfully requested to enlarge and publish, in book form, his essay on the History of Spiritualism, read before this Association, and that we hereby pledge ourselves to use our efforts to give circulation to said book."

The essay was subsequently read, by request, before an association of clergymen at Bridgewater, Mass., when the following resolution was passed:

"*Resolved*, That the thanks of this Association be tendered to Rev. W. M'Donald for his very able essay on the History of Spiritualism, and we concur with the Providence District Association in requesting its publication."

The essay has been enlarged to about four times its original size, thereby adding very much to the value of the book.

Our object has been, mainly, to prove that modern Spiritualism, claiming to be a "*New Dispensation*," is older than Christianity. It has generally appeared in connection with some remarkable religious movement, and always in conflict with it.

If Spiritualism be the work of spirits, they are such spirits or demons as the Greek and Roman sorcerers evoked; such as possessed the man among the tombs in the country of the Gadarenes; such as possessed the damsel who troubled Paul and Silas at Philippi; such as were present in the witchcraft of Europe and America.

If Spiritualism be the action of odylic force, as claimed by Rogers, Mahan, and others; or if it be an intermediate agent between spirit and matter, nearly answering to odylic force, as claimed by Dr. Samson; or if it be mere sleight of hand, deception, humbuggery, as claimed by Professor Mattison and those who think with him, then this odylic force, intermediate agent, sleight of hand, or humbuggery has produced in the past all the phenomena of modern Spiritualism.

We are frank to confess that we believe Spiritualism to be, in part at least, the work of *demons;* and that Paul accurately describes them in 1 Tim. iv, 1: "Now the Spirit speaketh expressly, that in the latter times some shall depart from the faith, giving heed to seducing spirits and doctrines of devils." This conclusion cannot be avoided if we have succeeded in proving that New Testament demonology and Greek and Roman sorcery are identical. Of this the reader must judge. But this is not the point which we have labored to establish in these pages. Whether it be the one or the other does not affect our argument.

Many of the facts here presented will be new to a large class of readers; and as a book of reference on the "History of Spiritualism," ancient and modern, it will be found valuable.

The chapter on the "*Fruits of Spiritualism*" is a very dark picture. We have simply permitted spiritualists, and those who have abandoned it, to speak for themselves.

It has cost us no small amount of labor to collect and arrange the materials for this volume. We could have written a much larger book with less labor.

Among the works which we have consulted, and from which we have received valuable aid, are the following:

The Bible.

Works of Josephus.

Clarke's, Scott's, Barnes's, Bush's, and Olshausen's Notes and Commentaries.

Brown's, Calmet's, Buck's, Watson's, and Kitto's Biblical and Theological Dictionaries.

Rollin's Ancient History.

Eusebius's Ecclesiastical History,

Du Pin's Ecclesiastical History.

Works of Dr. Dick.

Works of Dr. Stackhouse.

Works of Dr. Lardner.

Works of Dr. Lee.

Anthon's Classical Dictionary.

Arminian Magazine.

Encyclopedia Americana.

Wesley Family, by Dr. Adam Clarke.

Southey's Life of Wesley.

Witchcraft and Demonology, by Sir Walter Scott.

Magnalia Christi-Americana, by Cotton Mather, London, 1702.

Wonders of the Invisible World, by Cotton Mather, London, 1693.

More Wonders of the Invisible World, by Robert Calef, London, 1700.

History of Witchcraft, by Francis Hutchinson, D.D., London, 1718.

Massachusetts Historical Collections.

History of Magic, by Ennemoser, London.

Salem Witchcraft, by J. Thatcher.

Salem Witchcraft, by C. Upham.

London Retrospective Review.

Westminster Review.

Domestic Annals of Scotland, by Chambers.

Footfalls on the Boundaries of Another World, by Robert Dale Owen.

Spiritualism Tested, by George W. Samson, D.D.

Spirit Manifestations, by Rev. Charles Beecher.

Spirit Rappings, by Rev. J. Porter, D.D.

Ancient Sorcery Revived in Modern Spiritualism, by Rev. C. Munger.

Modern Mysteries Explained and Exposed, by President Mahan.

Modern Spiritualism, its Truths and its Errors, by Rev. T. L. Harris.

Spiritualism, Vols. I, II, by Judge Edmonds and Dr. Dexter.

Spiritualism Scientifically Demonstrated, by Robert Hare, M.D.

Rise and Progress of the Mysterious Noises in Western New York, by E. W. Capron and H. D. Barron.

The New Testament, as Corrected by the Spirits.

Ministry of Angels Realized, by Mr. and Mrs. Newton.

Spirit Works, Real but not Miraculous, by Allen Putnam.

Discussion of Modern Spiritualism, by Professor J. S. Grimes and Leo Miller, Esq.

History of the Supernatural, by W. Howitt.

Spiritual Telegraph.

Banner of Light.

We have had an opportunity of witnessing the phenomena of Spiritualism.

That this little volume may lead some soul, blinded by the God of this world, to Him who was revealed to destroy the works of the devil, and save many from falling who are halting between two opinions, is the earnest prayer of the author.

W. M'DONALD.

CONTENTS.

CHAPTER I.

SPIRITUALISM.

Hydesville Rappings — Dr. Hare — Mediums — Rapping, Tipping, etc.— Tables — Chairs — Piano-fortes — Guitars — House-bells — Clothing — Persons held and thrown down — Dr. Hare at Cape May — Writing — Speaking — New Dispensation — Its Theology.................................. Page 15

CHAPTER II.

ANCIENT SORCERY.

Terms employed and defined — Oracle of Trophonius — Oracle of Claros — Oracle of Apollo — Mediums — Poetical Mediums — Prophetic Mediums— Sealed Letters — Crœsus — Trajan — Jamblicus — Sibylline Oracles — Du Pin — Justin Martyr — Speaking Mediums — Healing Mediums — Temple of Æsculapius — Temple to Hygeia — Writing Mediums — Circles — Cicero — Æneas — Pliny — Apion — Achilles — Basic Fact of Spiritualism 31

CHAPTER III.

NEW TESTAMENT DEMONOLOGY.

Diabolos — Satanas — Daimon — Diamonion — Personified Principles of Evil — Personal Enemies — Diseases — Campbell — Lee — Damsel at Philippi — Kitto — Josephus — Lardner — Apollo — Simon Magus — Justin Martyr — Olshausen .... Page 54

CHAPTER IV.

MODERN WITCHCRAFT.

Witchcraft on the Continent — Germany — University of Paris — Norbonne — Pope John XXII. — Synod of Langress — Bull of Pope Innocent VIII. — Florimond — Number of Witches executed on the Continent — Joan of Arc — Sorcery in England and Scotland — Bishop Jewell — Laws of England — Numbers executed in England — Edmond Hartley — Laws of Scotland — Dr. Dick — Females — Bullingbrook — Maid of Kent — Miss Throgmorton — Meikle John Gibb — Mediums — Pordage and his Society of Angelic Brethren — Jane Lead — Revelations — Daughter of a Protestant Clergyman — Peter Apon — Blind Conjurer of Paris — Surrey Demoniac — Musical Mediums — Nuns of Loudou — Agnes Sympson — Bessie Dunlop and Thomas Reid — Alison Pearson and William Sympson — Compared with Spiritualism 75

CHAPTER V.

SALEM WITCHCRAFT.

When commenced — Dr. Bently — Judge Story — Boston — Springfield, etc. — Rev. Mr. Parris's Children — Witches —

Fast — The Court — Numbers accused — Numbers executed — The Reaction — Confession of Judges — Rev. Mr. Parris compelled to retire — Robert Calif's Book — Cotton and Increase Mather — Phenomena of Witchcraft — Ann Cole — William Morse — George Watson — Philip Smith — Children of John Goodwin — Thomas Brattle's Letter to the Salem Gentlemen — Mediums — Thatcher — Hutchinson — Dr. Sampson — Cotton Mather — Witchcraft compared with Spiritualism .... Page 95

CHAPTER VI

THE SPIRIT OF MASCON AND EPWORTH RAPPINGS.

Rev. Mr. Perreaud — Synod at Bussy — Noises commence — Curtain drawn — Pewter and Brass thrown about the Kitchen — Mr. Perreaud returns — Noises — Elders and others called in — Voice heard — Language used — Relates secret Matters — Mocks God — Tumbles the Bed — Music — Throwing Stones — Bishop of Mascon — Rev. J. Wesley — Robert Boyle — Rev. Peter du Molin — Epworth Rappings — Rev. S. Wesley — Knockings — Prayer for the King — Wesley thrice pushed — Rev. Mr. Hoole called in — Children disturbed while asleep — Dog affected — Footsteps heard — Groans — Trencher dances — Dr. Priestley — Mr. Southey — Coleridge — Dr. Adam Clarke — Spiritualism and Revivals of Religion 113

CHAPTER VII.

GOD'S TESTIMONY AGAINST SPIRITUALISM.

Rev. C. Munger — Divine Law — Sin of Babylon — Sin of Manasseh — Sin of Saul — Witch — Samuel — Rebellion — New Testament Law — Dr. Hare — Who consulted Spirits? 141

CHAPTER VIII.

FRUITS OF MODERN SPIRITUALISM.

Spiritualistic View of Revelation — Rev. T. L. Harris on Spiritualism — Sin — Dr. Hare — Lizzy Doten — Banner of Light — Christ — Banner of Light — Emma Harding — No Redeemer in the Spiritualist's Heaven — St. Stephen — St. John — Hell — Emma Harding — Lizzy Doten — Rich Man — Invocation to the Prince of Darkness — Invocation to Lucifer — Pagan Devil-worship — Marriage — Banner of Light .... Page 158

CHAPTER IX.

TESTIMONY AGAINST SPIRITUALISM.

W. Fishbough — W. B. Coan — B. F. Hatch, M.D. — J. F. Whiting — Cora L. V. Hatch — Wise Man's Counsel 191

SPIRITUALISM.

CHAPTER I.

SPIRITUALISM.

A BRIEF description of modern spiritualism in its *history*, *mediums*, *phenomena*, and *theology*, will aid us in our investigation of its general history. We shall be able the more readily to identify its present with its former phenomena.

In 1848 there lived in Hydesville, near Rochester, New York, a farmer by the name of John D. Fox. Mr. and Mrs. Fox were the parents of six children, the two youngest only—Margaret and Kate—living at home; the former fifteen, and the latter twelve years of age.

The house into which the family had recently removed was soon disturbed by noises, supposed to proceed from rats and mice. These noises, at first somewhat confused, were soon observed to be slight, but distinct knockings, in and about the bed-room, which gradually became louder and more general. The children were disturbed in bed by something resembling a dog lying on their feet, and a cold hand felt on Kate's face. Bedclothes were frequently pulled from the bed, chairs and tables removed from their places, and, in short, there was a general disarrangement of household matters.

Every effort was made by Mr. and Mrs. Fox to discover the cause of these strange disturbances, but without any satisfactory results.

On the night of March 31st, 1848, the parents and children lodged in the same room. At an early hour the rappings commenced with unusual violence. Thinking the noise might proceed from the rattling of the sashes, it being a windy night, Mr. Fox tried them, but found them all secure. Kate observed that when he shook the sashes, the noises responded; and turning in the direction from which the sounds proceeded, snapped her finger, and exclaimed, "Here, old Splitfoot, do as I do." The knockings instantly responded.

These manifestations of apparent intelligence so alarmed the girls that they desisted for a time from trying any more experiments.

Mrs. Fox seemed anxious to go further, and did so. She soon learned the ages of her children, and something of the history of the spirit which communicated with her. His name was Charles B. Rosma, a married man, the father of five children, and thirty-one years old. He had been murdered there some years before by one John C. Bell, a blacksmith, and his remains buried in the cellar of the house, at a depth of ten feet. This intelligence produced unheard-of excitement in the town, and the people flocked from all parts to hear and see. Excavations were made in the cellar at different times, as the water would allow. At the depth of five feet they found plank: further on, pieces of crockery, charcoal, and quick lime;

then human hair, and bones said by anatomists to have been portions of a human skeleton.

These are among the alleged facts connected with this case. There were many contradictory statements made, but it does not come within our province to examine them in this brief treatise.

The rappings were not confined to the Fox residence, but were soon heard in other houses in the neighborhood; and not long after they appeared in Rochester, and the adjoining towns and cities; and now we find them everywhere.

In this simple manner commenced what are known as the "Rochester Knockings."

Dr. Hare says he inquired of his "*spirit-father*" why these manifestations were first made at Hydesville, through the spirit of a murdered man? and his father informed him that Hydesville was chosen because of the ignorance of the people, and the spirit of a murdered man was employed because that would excite more interest. (Spiritualism Scientifically Demonstrated, p. 85.)

Here is the origin of modern mediumship; and it is wonderful with what rapidity mediums have multiplied since Kate Fox first introduced herself to "old Splitfoot" at Hydesville, in 1848.

The mediums of modern spiritualism may be classified as follows:

1. *Rapping Mediums*, who produce distinct sounds by the aid of unseen agents.

2. *Tipping Mediums*, who move tables, and household furniture generally, with all kinds of material substances.

3. *Speaking Mediums*, who pronounce discourses, under the inspiration, professedly, of departed spirits, equal in all respects, if not superior, as they claim, to any ever pronounced by mortals.

4. *Seeing Mediums*, who claim to be able to clearly see and accurately describe invisible spirits.

5. *Drawing Mediums*, who furnish drawings of leaves, vines, fruit and flowers of the spirit-land, which cannot be classified by human botanists.

6. *Painting Mediums*, who in thirty minutes, it is said, can furnish full-length portraits of persons long since dead; which, in point of artistic skill, equals Michael Angelo, Correggio, Raphael, or Titian.

7. *Musical Mediums*, who discourse exquisite music on piano-fortes, guitars, and, in fact, all kinds of instruments, without the aid of fleshly fingers.

8. *Singing Mediums*, whose vocal performances are quite up to Jenny Lind.

9. *Dancing Mediums*, whose performances in this department throw Ellen Tree, Fanny Ellsler, or the most accomplished French dancing-master entirely into the shade.

10. *Writing Mediums*, who are filling the land with volumes dictated by departed spirits.

11. *Healing Mediums*, who claim to cure the most obstinate diseases by prescriptions furnished by the departed. These prescriptions are said to produce wonders, of which the "waters of Israel" and "balm of Gilead" could never boast.

12. *Developing Mediums*, whose operations are a little obscure, and hence not so easily described.

These are the more prominent *mediums* of Spiritualism, from which the extent of mediumship among them may be learned.

The general facts of Spiritualism are so well attested, that few persons are found, whatever their opinion of the phenomena, who are willing to risk their reputation for candor on an unqualified denial of them. There may be a difference of opinion as to the force or agent by which these phenomena are produced; but that they are produced, and that, too, in many cases, without deception, cannot be successfully questioned.

Among these facts may be mentioned the following:

Tables have been raised from the floor, and carried into different parts of a room without visible human aid, while herculean efforts were being made to arrest them. President Mahan mentions several well-attested cases of tables moved in every possible direction, and with great force; of a table seen to rise from the floor, and to float in the atmosphere for several seconds; of a table, on which was seated a Mr. Wells, rocking to and fro with great violence, and at length poising itself on two legs, and remaining in that position for some thirty seconds, with no other person in contact with it. (Modern Mysteries Explained, etc., pp. 112, 113.)

Chairs and other articles of furniture have been seen to deliberately move about a house, unimpelled by visible human agency, and in many instances have been known to be broken into fragments.

Piano-fortes have discoursed the sweetest music, with their key-boards pressed closely to the wall, and no human hand upon the keys. I have received such statements from the lips of credible witnesses, persons who at present have no connection with Spiritualism.

Guitars have repeatedly discoursed music quite as sweet, while moving around a room without human aid. In Auburn, N. Y., in the presence of many witnesses, a guitar is said to have been "taken from the hands of those who held it and *put in tune*, and to have commenced playing while it passed around the room above their heads."—*History of Mysterious Noises*, p. 72.

"A very intelligent Christian lady," says President Mahan, "an utter disbeliever in Spiritualism, told us, that in her presence a guitar was once placed in the middle of the room; that when no one was within several feet of it, musical sounds proceeded from it," etc.—*Modern Mysteries*, etc., p. 117.

House-bells have been lifted from their places and rung over the heads of numerous spectators. This is quite common. Judge Edmonds speaks of such matters frequently. On one occasion he says, "The bell was taken out of M.'s hand and rung, and then put back again. This occurred several times in the course of the evening." Again, he says, "The bell was rung over our heads," etc.—*Spiritualism*, vol. i, pp. 22, 23, 26.

Articles of clothing have been snatched from

the persons of many by an unseen hand, and in the presence of many witnesses.

The author last mentioned speaks of a shawl being "snatched from a lady's shoulders, and thrown on the floor."—P. 24.

Many similar cases might be named.

Some have been nearly thrown upon the floor, and others have been arrested and firmly held by an invisible agent. Says Judge Edmonds, "Some were pulled down upon the sofa; one was pulled nearly on to the floor; one had her feet shoved from under her, so that she nearly fell." "One of the party was forcibly torn by an invisible power from my grasp, in spite alike of his strength and mine." "I felt on one of my arms what seemed to be the grip of an iron hand. I felt distinctly the thumb and fingers, the palm of the hand, and the ball of the thumb; and it held me fast by a power which I struggled to escape from in vain. No earthly hand could thus have held me, for I was as powerless in that grip as a fly would be in the grasp of my hand. And it continued with me until I had tried every means I could devise to get rid of it; and not until I thoroughly felt how powerless I was, did it leave me."—*Spiritualism*, vol. i, pp. 24, 26, 27.

Responses by rapping and writing have been received to mental questions, known only to the inquirer. Facts unknown to the parties at the time, and many facts regarded *false* at the time, have subsequently proved to be as stated by the medium.

Dr. Hare states that he sent a message by a spirit, from Cape May to Philadelphia, with regard to bank business of which he was uncertain. The spirit communicated with Mrs. Gourlay, of Philadelphia, through whose husband the proper inquiries were made at the bank, and the answer returned to Dr. Hare, by the same spirit, all in two hours and a half. Such facts are quite numerous.

The *facsimile* of a handwriting the medium had never seen has been produced; while paper has been written upon with pen and ink, when it is known that no human being was in the room at the time; neither was there pen nor ink present. Not only do we find many such statements in the productions of spiritualists, but we have received them from the lips of those who, having formerly been connected with spiritualism, had abandoned it.

Mediums have pronounced such discourses, as it is known they never did nor could pronounce in a normal state.

Persons are said to have been restored to health by prescriptions purporting to come from the spirits of departed physicians.

These are a few of the facts of Spiritualism. The list might be greatly extended, including many more marvelous than we have mentioned.

Spiritualism claims to be a religious system. It has its altars, its priests, its Church services, and revelations. It goes further, and lays claim to being a New Dispensation.

Judge Edmonds says: "As under the Mosaic Dispensation mankind were taught the existence of God, rather than the thousand gods with mortal attributes then worshiped; and under the Christian dispensation they were taught the immortality of the soul and its existence forever; so now, under *this new dispensation* it is being revealed to them, for the first time, what that state of existence is, and how, in this life, they may well and wisely prepare to enter upon" it.—Vol. i, p. 65.

He further says: "As came the dispensation through Christ, so came this, in a state of almost universal peace," etc.—P. 66.

Dr. Hare shouts over it: "Praise be to God that he has sent us a new way of religious light."—*Spiritualism*, etc., p. 208.

To the "New Testament, as Corrected by the Spirits," a new book is added, entitled, "*New Dispensation*," which begins thus:

"I, Jesus, appeared in spirit in 1861, and do say and declare unto the world that the new era or dispensation has commenced, called the coming of Christ. It commenced about the year 1847, and as represented and spoken of by the prophet Daniel and others, by my coming as a cloud in the heavens, with tens of thousands of angels, to overshadow the earth with my glory."

"We are called to witness," says the Banner of Light, "the beginning of a New Era in the history of Man."

"I expected of it (Spiritualism) as I would of the advent of a Jesus Christ."—*Banner of Light*, January 18, 1862.

Speaking of *perfection*, a spirit says: "But the new dispensation gives a new definition to all things, and therefore to perfection."—*Banner of Light*, March 8, 1862.

It denies the divine authority of the Bible, claiming superiority for its own revelations.

It denies the divinity of Christ, regarding him as a medium only, still progressing in the spheres.

It denies the atonement, claiming that man only needs development.

It has no redemption through Christ, no salvation by faith, no gracious regeneration by the Spirit.

It has no resurrection from the dead, no eternal judgment.

With Spiritualism, the God of the Bible was a ferocious spirit, more nearly representing our ideas of a devil than a God.

It claims that all human actions are in such a sense the result of necessity, as that no man could have acted differently from what he has done.

It claims that sin is an impossibility, and that vice is virtue under another name.

It is claimed that hell is the ante-chamber to heaven, and all must pass through hell to reach heaven. Such, in brief, are some of the facts and teachings of Spiritualism.

We shall have occasion to speak in another place of the character and fruits of this system, when its theology and morals will be more fully considered.

We are now prepared to show that this strange system, instead of being a *New Dispensation*, as claimed by its chief supporters, is older than Christianity, and has had its periodical developments in the past, and has been always found fighting against God, and Jesus Christ whom he 'has sent. To this examination we call special attention in the following pages.

CHAPTER II.

ANCIENT SORCERY.

It will be admitted that the distinguishing characteristic of modern Spiritualism is its professed intercourse with the spirits of the dead. Indeed, its advocates claim that in the process of human development this intercourse with the spirit-world is an advance on any former dispensation. But so far from Spiritualism being a new dispensation, we are prepared to show that the Greeks and Romans, before the establishment of Christianity, could boast of intercourse with the spirit-world, through their oracles, equal to anything yet seen in modern Spiritualism.

The terms employed to describe this commerce are, *necromancy*, *sorcery*, *witchcraft*, *magic*, *enchantment*, *divination*, *familiar spirits*, etc.

A definition of these terms will throw some light upon this subject.

1. "*Necromancy*," says Dr. Stackhouse, "is the art of raising up the dead in order to pry into future events, or to be informed of the fate of the living." Calmet says "it consisted in raising up the ghosts of individuals deceased." Buck says it is "the art of revealing future events by conversing with the dead."

"*Necromancers*," says Campbell, "are those who consult the dead." Dr. Lowth says they "are those who consult with evil spirits." Brown says they "were those who pretended to raise and consult with such persons as were dead." Dr. Jahn says, "necromancers pretended that they were able by their incantations to summon back departed spirits from their abodes. They uttered the communications which they pretended to receive from the dead."

If Stackhouse, and Calmet, and Buck, and Campbell, and Lowth, and Brown, and Jahn, have correctly defined necromancy, what is it but modern Spiritualism? or, what is modern Spiritualism but ancient necromancy?

2. "*Sorcerers*," says Gesenius, "are those who profess to call up the dead." "Sorcery," says Dr. Webster, is "the power of commanding evil spirits."

3. "*Magic*," says Calmet, is "the invocation of the devil." Dr. Webster says it "is the science of producing wonderful effects by the aid of superhuman beings, or of departed spirits."

4. "*Witchcraft* comprehends," says Brown, "all kinds of influence produced by collusion with Satan." Burkett says it is a "devilish art." Dr. Webster says, "it is intercourse with the dead."

5. "*Enchantment*," says Dr. Webster, "is the art of producing certain wonderful effects by the invocation or aid of demons, or the agency of certain supposed spirits." "An *enchanter* is one who has spirits or demons at his command; one who practices enchantment, or pretends to perform surprising things

3

by the agency of demons." Brown says they are such as "pretended to work things wonderful by superhuman influence."

6. "*Divination*," says Dr. Stackhouse, "is being in league and covenant with the devil, and doing many astonishing things by his help." "To divine, ordinarily signifies," says Brown, "to find out and foretell secret or future things by some sinful and diabolical means." "A diviner," says Dr. Webster, "is one who pretends to predict events, or to reveal occult things, by the aid of superior beings, or of supernatural means."

7. *Familiar spirit*, or the word *familiar* applied to *spirit*, says Mr. Barnes, is the word the Hebrews "used particularly to denote one who was supposed to have power to call up the dead, to learn of them respecting future events." Isa. viii, 19. Brown says, "*familiar spirits* are such devils as converse with wizards, and the like." Dr. Webster says, "a *familiar spirit* is a demon, or evil spirit, supposed to attend at a call."

Mr. Benson says, "the spirits of dead men were supposed to speak in the images or idols worshiped by the heathen."

Mr. Barnes says: "Among heathen nations, nothing was more common than for persons to profess to have intercourse with spirits, and to be under the influence of their inspiration."

"It was the opinion of many," says Dr. Lardner, "that evil angels and spirits were allowed to visit the region of our air and this earth, and to inflict diseases and other calamities upon men."

It is very clear that the ancient sorcerers, necromancers, enchanters, etc., professed to do all that modern spiritualists profess to do. They profess to perform their wonders by the aid of superhuman or spiritual beings. They claimed that the spirits which aided them were the spirits of their demigods, heroes, and departed friends. We shall see, in the course of this examination, that their claim is as well founded as that of spiritualists.

Identical in character with the necromancers,

sorcerers, etc., mentioned in the Scriptures, were the priests of the oracles of Greece and Rome.

These oracles were the pagan deities who gave, or were supposed to give, answers to inquiries made respecting affairs of importance, usually respecting future events, and the success of important enterprises. They were quite numerous.

The oracle of Trophonius was held in high repute. The mediums, when in the trance state, had revealed to them, it is said, much of futurity. Some are said to have been seeing mediums, and could describe by sight; while others were hearing mediums, and described what they heard. They became stupefied, and out of their senses. They were then placed in the chair of the goddess of memory, and by her aid were enabled to relate what they had seen and heard. These efforts, it is said, produced great physical prostration.

The oracle of Claros was remarkable for its poetical genius. It could, among other remarkable things, deliver answers in verse upon what persons had in their thoughts, though often very ignorant, and knowing nothing of composing in rhyme. This oracle is said to have foretold the sudden death of Germanicus, the accomplished Roman general.

Passing over a large number of inferior oracles, we come to consider the most famous one of all antiquity, the oracle of Apollo at Delphos, worshiped under the name of Pythian; so called from the serpent Python, or from the Greek word *puthesthai*, which signifies *to inquire*, because the people came there to consult him. From thence the Delphic priestess was called Pythia, and the games were celebrated and known as the Pythian games.

Diodorus says that there was a cavity upon Parnassus from which exhalations arose producing wonderful effects. On approaching it the brain became intoxicated, and even beasts were seriously affected by it. A shepherd approaching it was seized with violent agitations of body, and pronounced words which he did not understand, but words said to have foretold futurity. The influence was regarded as something divine, and a priestess—a woman of course—was appointed to receive and transmit the divine communications. These priestesses were nothing more or less than trance-mediums, with which Spiritualism abounds. They multiplied with great rapidity, and the people flocked from all quarters to inquire of them, either by word of mouth or in writing, with regard to the secret things of the present and future.

Under the influence of the miraculous vapor, "the hair of the priestess," says Rollin, "stood upright upon her head; her look grew wild and furious; she foamed at the mouth, while a sudden and violent trembling seized her whole body, with all the symptoms of distraction and frenzy."

Virgil, referring to the same thing, says,

> "The virgin cries, The god! behold the god!
> And straight her visage and her color change;
> Her hair disheveled, and her heaving breast
> And laboring heart are swollen with sacred rage;
> Larger she seems; her voice, no mortal sound,
> As the inspiring god, near and more near,
> Seizes her soul."

Virgil says again,

> "She fetched up souls out of their tomb."

And again,

> "She raiseth souls out of their graves."

This description by Virgil of the priestess of Apollo so accurately portrays the spiritualistic mediums of the present day that comment is unnecessary.

We have said there were poetical mediums, who delivered the communications of the oracles in verse.

These verses are said to have been very bad, at least in many instances; so much so that many were much surprised that Apollo, who presided in the choir of the Muses, by whom these verses were supposed to have been inspired, should have been so bad a rhymer. But Plutarch defends Apollo, and claims that he did not compose the verses of the medium, but simply inflamed her imagination, and kindled in her soul that living light which unvailed all of futurity to her. The substance of the communications was inspired, while the manner of expressing it was left to the genius and natural talent of the medium. He says,

"The first inspiration alone comes from him, (Apollo,) which is, however, adapted to the nature of every prophetess. Therefore, voice and sound, expression and meter, do not belong to Apollo, but to the woman; he only inspires her with the images and conceptions, and inflames her soul so that it can see the future."—*History of Magic*, vol. i, p. 416.

It is very remarkable that spiritualists employ Plutarch's reasoning to meet the objections urged against the genuineness of many modern communications purporting to come from persons remarkable for their good sense while in the body.

Take the following samples of poetic genius, communicated, professedly, by Washington and Franklin. The first is Washington, drawing his own portrait in verse. (Love and Wisdom, from the Spirit World.)

"When the likeness of this portrait you see,
Remember that it is to represent the likeness of me;

But the spirit in its brightness you cannot see,
For that is far above the likeness of thee."

Here follows some lines composed by the great mind of Franklin, after some seventy years' residence in his "angels' home:"

"The likeness of this portrait is to represent
The likeness of man when he dwelt here below;
But the likeness of the spirit you would like to know,
As this would be no more than I would like to show;
But the mind is not prepared the likeness for to see
Of the spirit in his angel's home as bright as we."

If Apollo's mediums succeeded in grinding out meaner poetry than this, they needed a Plutarch to defend them.

Judge Edmonds offers the same explanation for modern mediums that Plutarch does for the ancient. He says, "The visions which I have are impressed on my mind as vividly and distinctly as any material object can be; yet in giving them to others, I must rely upon and use my own powers of observation, my own memory, my own command of language. At other times the thought is given me sentence by sentence, and I know not what idea or sentence is to follow; but the language used is my own, and is selected by myself from my own memory's storehouse. At other times the whole current of thought or process of reasoning is given me in advance, and I choose for myself the language and the illustrations used to convey it, and sometimes the order of giving it. But in all these modes there is more or less of myself in them, more or less of my individuality underlying it all." "I have noticed the same thing in the doctor." (G. T. Dexter.) "The main idea might be transmitted correctly enough, but it would be liable to various shadings, from the different capacity of the messengers to comprehend it, and from the variety of their power of language to utter it."—*Spiritualism*, vol. ii, pp. 39, 40, 43.

How perfectly does Judge Edmond's defense of the mediums of modern Spiritualism agree with Plutarch's defense of the oracles of Greece.

There were many who questioned the ability of the oracles to foretell future events, or accurately describe what was transpiring at a distance. To detect what they regarded as imposition, resort was had to stratagem; and "it must be confessed," says Rollin, "that sometimes the answer of the oracles was clear and circumstantial."

The wealthy Crœsus, King of Lydia, sent his embassador and demanded of the oracle to inform him what he was doing at a given time. The oracle of Delphos replied that he was causing a tortoise and a lamb to be dressed in a vessel of brass, which was really so.

The Emperor Trajan made a like demand of the oracle at Heliopolis, by sending a sealed letter, to which he demanded an answer. The oracle replied by sending to the emperor a bit of blank paper nicely folded and sealed. Trajan was amazed to find the answer in perfect harmony with the letter sent, which contained nothing but blank paper.

"It was customary," says Rollin, "to consult the oracles by sealed letters, which were laid upon the altar of the god unopened."

It was claimed that demons moved the fluids, both of the interior and exterior senses, and thus presented to the organs certain forms, just as they would outwardly meet us, not only in sleep, but when awake. "Thus demons do really affect us," they say, "and communicate knowledge."—*Spiritualism Tested.*

Jamblicus, a Platonic philosopher and disciple of Porphyry, in the third century, wrote a treatise on the subject of spiritual mysteries among the Egyptians, Chaldeans, and Assyrians, in which he gives a brief description of a spiritualistic medium of these times, which will be recognized as a correct representation of a modern medium:

"Some are agitated throughout the whole body; others, in some of their members; others, again, are entirely quiet. Sometimes there are pleasing harmonies, dances, and according-voices, and sometimes the reverse. Again, the body either appears taller, or larger, or is borne aloft through the air, or is affected by the opposite of these."

Again, "Inspiration is the work neither of soul nor body, nor of their entire compound. The true cause is no other than illumination emanating from the very gods themselves, and spirits coming forth from them, and an obsession by which they hold us fully and absolutely, absorbing all our faculties even, and exterminating all human motions and operations, even to consciousness itself; bringing discourses which they who utter them do not understand, but pronounce with furious lip, so that our whole being becomes secondary, and subservient to the sole power of the occupying god."—*Beecher*, pp. 38, 39.

The *Sibylline oracles*, or *verses*, are of the same character.

The ancients represent the Sibyl as a woman endowed with a prophetic spirit, and roving from country to country, vending her predictions, which were nothing more than the productions of writing mediums. They were somewhat numerous in various parts of Greece and other places. Their predictions were usually delivered in verse, and contained, it is said, accounts of heaven, hell, and the condition of the dead. They were highly esteemed. The Sibyl of Cumo wrote her predictions on the leaves of a tree. They were sold to the king of the Romans, who caused them to be carefully laid up in an urn, or stone pot, in the capital, and officers placed over them. In this manner superhuman knowledge is said to have been sought among the Romans.

Speaking of these mediums, the historian Du Pin says, "They were transported with enthusiasm and extravagant fury, caused by the possession of demons." Inspiration was claimed for them; but he remarks, "we need only read the description that is made of all the ancient oracles. It was so evident among the heathen that they were possessed, that they applied the word to them which signified, "to play the madman."

"Now this fury that deprived them of their senses cannot be esteemed as an inspiration of the Holy Ghost, but as an effect of their being possessed with demons."—*Eccles. Hist.*, p. 18.

Justin Martyr says, "The Sibyl was born at Babylon, and came thence to Cumo, where she revealed future things. She speaks great and wonderful things, knowing not herself what she says. When she begins to lose the inspiring spirit, she loses at the same time the memory of all that she has foretold."

Healing Mediums were very numerous, and are said to have performed wonders in that line.

Under the reign of Claudius, the temple of Æsculapius, son of the famous Apollo, and god of the healing art, was so celebrated on account of the cures there performed, that it became a place of general resort for the sick. Masters sent their slaves thither to be healed; and by a decree of the emperor, all so healed became free.

In Nero's time these consultations in the temple were very common. Pliny gives some of the curative means recommended.

A temple was erected by Junius Bubulcus

to Hygeia, daughter of Æsculapius, and goddess of health. (History of Magic, vol. i, p. 435.) Marvelous were the cures she is said to have wrought. From this originated the term *Hygiene:* meaning, "That department of medicine which treats of the preservation of health."—*Webster.*

"The stoic hints that wonders of healing, and strange powers of reading and writing, accompanied the influence."—*Spiritualism Tested,* p. 86.

"Its relation to medicine," says President Samson, "gave it its first grasp on human life."

"Circles" were as common then as they are now.

In speaking of mercenary soothsaying, Cicero says, "I have no confidence in fortune-tellers, mercenary soothsayers, nor *circles.*" It is very remarkable that the word here rendered "circle" [psychomantium] means precisely what is meant by a modern spiritualistic circle—"a place where one inquires anything of the spirits of the dead." For what purpose are spiritual circles established, but to inquire of the spirits of the dead?"

In speaking of real soothsaying, Cicero says:

"They believe that in the spirit of man dwells an oracle, by which the future may be perceived, either when the soul is excited by divine inspiration, or when through sleep the soul expands herself unfettered."—*History of Magic*, p. 137.

The Trojan Æneas goes in confident devosion to the cave of the Cumean sybil, where spirits communicate with mortals. The sibyl displays wonderful knowledge of his family. Through this medium he receives communications from the shade or spirit of his father Anchises. These communications are said to have been received by the sibyl when in sleeping vision or magnetic trance; for "from the ivory gate of sleep Anchises at last releases them."

Of the various methods by which knowledge of spiritual things was gained, Pliny mentions "conversation with disembodied spirits and inferior deities." He speaks of Apion, who declared that he himself had called up departed spirits, in order to inquire of Homer of what country and what ancestors he was born; while, nevertheless, he did not dare to publish what he had replied. (Spiritualism Tested, p. 81.)

Achilles is said to have been first thoroughly convinced of the reality of the future life and the spirit-world when the shade of Patroclus, his slaughtered friend, appeared to him. He felt the hand and saw the glistening eye of the goddess Minerva checking him. (Spiritualism Tested, p. 90.)

Let no one imagine that we are writing of the faith and practice of modern Spiritualism from the facts witnessed around us daily; we are describing scenes which were witnessed two thousand years ago. But who does not see in this description of ancient sorcery a full-length portrait of modern Spiritualism? What is the boast of modern Spiritualism over the sorcery and magic of the ancients? Does Spiritualism lay as its foundation stone intercourse with the spirit-world?

The "Banner of Light" for Dec. 28, 1861, says, "The basic fact of Spiritualism is the belief that certain phenomena, occurring in a way that renders them impossible to be the result of human action, are produced by an intelligent though invisible agency. That the intelligence communicated is identical with certain deceased persons; hence, that the agency is human, spiritual, and actually proceeds from the disembodied souls of mortals."

But is not this the "basic fact" of ancient necromancy? The whole system was built upon this "fact;" hence Spiritualism, in its "basic fact," is but a reproduction of the old magic. This is progress with a vengeance! This is your boasted new light! Does Spiritualism claim to foretell what is yet to be? A prophetic spirit is their boast. But does not this also find its counterpart in ancient sorcery? They have recorded as many wonders in this regard as Spiritualism can boast of.

Does Spiritualism boast of a multiplicity of mediums—speaking, writing, seeing, healing, and developing? Ancient sorcery could boast of as great a variety. They had their oracle at Delphos, whose prince was Beelzebub; their vessels of fury, whose prince was Belial; their revenging devils, whose prince was Asmodeus; their *cozens*, who belonged to magicians and witches, whose prince was Satan; their aerial demons, who caused plagues, thunder, and fire, whose prince was Merison; their captain of the furies, causing wars, tumults, and uproars, whose prince was Abaddon; their calumniating demons, driving men into despair, whose prince was Daiabolas; their several kinds of tempting demons, whose prince was Mammon. They could speak, and write, and heal the sick, and see the future, as much to the satisfaction of the people then living as Spiritualists do in these days. The old magic has simply arisen from the dead, and therefore mighty works do show forth themselves in it. They had their circles, their lectures, and their physical manifestations then, as these have them now. Spiritualism has simply left the light of Christianity and the Book of God's counsels, and gone back two or three thousand years into pagan darkness; proving that word true, "If our light become darkness, how great is that darkness."

Men who wish to advance backward into Paganism can do so by embracing modern Spiritualism.

CHAPTER III.

NEW TESTAMENT DEMONOLOGY.

THE subject of *New Testament Demonology* has long been a fruitful topic of discussion, producing no little confusion in the common mind. We shall enter into this discussion just far enough to present the subject in a clear light, and present such facts as shall go to identify it with the Spiritualism of these times.

There are four words employed in the New Testament, rendered in our English version *Satan* and *devil.* We call the reader's attention to the import of these words, in order to a proper understanding of the subject.

1. *Diabolos.* This word signifies, according to Robinson, "traducer, accuser, slanderer, devil." It occurs thirty-eight times in the New Testament, and in every case save four is beyond all doubt applied to the prince of fallen

angels. The exceptions are John vi, 70, where Judas is called a *devil;* 1 Tim. iii, 11, where the word is rendered *slanderers;* 2 Tim. iii, 3, and Titus ii, 3, where it is rendered *false accusers.*

"But nothing is easier," says Campbell, "than to distinguish this application from the more frequent application to the arch-apostate. One mark of distinction is that, in this last use of the term, it is never found in the plural. When the plural is used, the context always shows that it is human beings, and not fallen angels, that are spoken of." "Another criterion, whereby the application of this word to the prince of darkness may be discovered, is its being attended with the article."—*Dissertation* VI, vol. i, p. 241.

As examples of the use of *Diabolos*, we mention the following:

"Then was Jesus led up of the Spirit into the wilderness to be tempted of the devil." Matt. iv, 1. "The enemy that sowed them is the devil," Matt. xiii, 39. "Depart from me, ye cursed, into everlasting fire, prepared for the devil and his angels." Matt. xxv, 41. "Resist the devil and he will flee from you." James iv, 7. "He that committeth sin is of the devil." 1 John iii, 8.

Let it be remembered that *Diabolos* is never applied to those New Testament demons cast out by Christ and the apostles. Another term is used, as we shall see, when they are spoken of.

2. *Satanas*, or *Satan*. This is a Hebrew word, introduced into New Testament Greek compositions. In Hebrew, according to Gesenius, it means, "an adversary, an enemy, Satan;" and according to Robinson, it is the Hebrew proper name for the devil. It never occurs in the plural. Though we frequently read of devils, we never read of Satans, from which we infer that it denotes the chief of evil spirits or devils. It is used about thirty times in the New Testament. As examples of its use, take the following:

"Satan cometh and taketh away the word that was sown in their hearts." Mark iv, 15.

"I beheld Satan as lightning fall from heaven." Luke x, 18.

"And after the sop, Satan entered into him." John xiii, 27

"Why hath Satan filled thine heart to lie to the Holy Ghost." Acts v, 3.

"And the God of peace shall bruise Satan under your feet shortly." Rom. xvi, 20.

"Satan himself is transformed into an angel of light." 2 Cor. xi, 14.

"And he laid hold on the dragon, that old serpent, which is the devil and Satan." Rev. xx, 2.

These are sufficient to show the use made of this term by the inspired writers. It will be seen that this, too, is not the word employed by them when speaking of the spirits or devils cast out by Christ and the apostles.

3. *Daimon.* According to Robinson, this word, in its New Testament meaning, signifies "a demon, an evil spirit, devil." It occurs only five times in the New Testament; once in each of the Gospels of Matthew, Mark, and Luke, and twice in the Apocalypse. In the three Gospels it refers to the same possession—the man in

the country of the Gadarenes, who haunted the sepulchers. It occurs also in Rev. xvi, 14: "For they are the spirits of devils." Rev. xviii, 2, Babylon "is become the habitation of devils."

4. *Daimonion.* This word is derived from the one last mentioned, and has the same meaning. In fact they are used interchangeably in the New Testament.

When a devil or devils are said to have been cast out by Christ, these [daimon and daimonion] are the terms employed to denote the being who was cast out. They are called demons, or devils, according to our translation. This word occurs about sixty times in the New Testament, and is not once confounded with *diabolos*, which occurs thirty-eight times, showing that the beings denoted by these two terms are not the same. "But what sets the difference of signification in the clearest light," says Campbell, "is that, though both words, *diabolos* and *daimonion*, occur often in the Septuagint, they are invariably used for translating different Hebrew words. *Diabolos* is always in Hebrew either *tsar*, enemy, or *Satan*, adversary; words never translated *daimonion*. This latter word, on the contrary, is made to express some Hebrew term signifying idol, pagan deity, apparition, or what some render satyr."

There is but one passage in the New Testament in which this word is not rendered *devil*. The exception is Acts xvii, 18, "He seemeth to be a setter forth of strange gods." Here the term is rendered *gods*, and is so used in harmony with the faith of the heathen Greeks, who regarded the demon as a deity, a god, good or bad.

As examples of the New Testament use of daimonion, we submit the following:

"And he healed many that were sick of divers diseases, and cast out many devils; and suffered not the devils to speak, because they knew him." Mark i, 34.

"But the Pharisees said, He casteth out devils through the prince of the devils." Matt. ix, 34.

"And devils also came out of many." Luke iv, 41.

"Can a devil open the eyes of the blind?" John x, 20.

"The devils also believe and tremble." John ii, 19.

Every one must see at a glance that *daimonion* does not apply to the prince of devils, or Satan proper, but to an inferior or subordinate class of devils.

It has been claimed that these demons were not spiritual beings; but that in some texts nothing more is meant than a personified principle of evil; in others, the evil propensity in human nature; in others, personal enemies; in others, diseases, such as madness, or violent insanity. There seems to be no uniform method of scriptural interpretation among those who deny the existence of devils. But it requires more faith than we are in possession of to believe that the inspired writers could have used language so vaguely. It must be admitted that if the existence of demons is denied, no common sense explanation can be given of demoniac possessions; and no one can successfully vindicate the writers of the New Testament against the charge of being either ignorant of their subject, or of lacking a knowledge of the proper terms to set it forth.

"When I find mention made of the number of demons in particular possessions, their actions expressly distinguished from those of the man possessed; conversations held by the former about the disposal of them after their expulsion, and accounts given how they were actually disposed of; when I find desires and passions ascribed peculiarly to them, and similitudes taken from the conduct which they usually observe, it is impossible for me to deny their existence, without admitting that the sacred historians were either deceived themselves in regard to them, or intended to deceive their readers."—*Campbell*, vol. i, p. 252.

If you call these demons a personified principle of evil, you encounter the facts of a legion of these evil principles entering into one man, and that these personified principles of evil were transferred from men to hogs;

proving, as Dr. Lee very justly remarks, that "hogs for once actually possessed human depravity."

If you call them diseases, which most persons who deny real possessions are inclined to do, you encounter the difficulty that when these diseases are about to be cast out, they express an earnest desire not to be sent out of the country, preferring to go into the swine, which request is granted. That must have been a complicated disease of which a legion are cast out of one man, and seven go out of one woman.

If you say that by devils is meant insanity, you will encounter the difficulty of a legion of insanities entering into one man, and then transferred from the man to swine, at their own request.

The New Testament writers clearly distinguish between diseases of all kinds, and devils, or, as they are sometimes termed, "unclean spirits." Two texts must suffice.

Matt. iv, xxix, "And they brought unto

him all sick people that were taken with divers diseases and torments, and those which were possessed with devils, and those which were lunatic, and those that had the palsy, and he healed them." From this scripture we learn that being possessed of devils was not being sick with divers diseases and torments, nor was it being a lunatic, a madman. What could it have been to answer the description of the writer?

Mark i, xxxiv, "And he healed many that were sick of divers diseases, and cast out many devils; and suffered not the devils to speak, because they knew him."

The additional facts in this case are the knowledge displayed by the demons, and the disposition which they manifested to speak. They knew Jesus, and on that account he suffered them not to speak. If these possessions were diseases, then diseases have intelligence, volition, and the power of speech.

All this was done in the presence of a people who firmly believed in the reality of demoniacal possessions. Now, if Christ did not cast out real devils, he deceived the people by practicing a solemn farce before them.

"An appeal may be made," says Rev. L. Lee, "to common sense, that the insanity, if there be any insanity in the case, must be with the writer, he who gave such an account of the cure of an insane person, or with the reader, who understands the history of the case to be an account of the cure of an insane man."—*Theology*, p. 236.

Take the account given of the damsel possessed of a spirit of divination, who troubled Paul and his companions at Philippi; also, the account given of the sons of Sceva attempting to cast out a demon, after the manner of Paul's casting them out at Ephesus. That was a strange disease which exclaimed, "Jesus I know, and Paul I know, but who are ye?"

But it may be asked, Where is the evidence that these possessions were the same as the sorcery of the Greeks, Romans, etc.? In order to answer this inquiry, let us inquire into the belief of the Jews on the subject, and the treatment of that belief by Christ and the Apostles.

Dr. Kitto says, "It was the general belief of the Jewish nation, except the Sadducees, and of most other nations, that the spirits of dead men," especially the wicked, were permitted to enter the bodies of men.

Josephus, who may be regarded as a safe expositor of Jewish opinion on this subject, says, "Demons are the spirits of wicked men, who enter into living men, and destroy them, unless they are so happy as to meet with speedy relief."

Drs. Lardner and Jahn, though disposed to question the real existence of demons, admit that the Jews believed this dogma.

Dr. Whedon says, "That evil spirits are permitted in some ages of gross wickedness to possess men has been the doctrine of the Church in all ages, until the cavils of some modern thinkers, more skeptical than wise, brought it in question."—*Notes*, Matt. iv, 24.

It is admitted that the term demon, applied by the Greeks to their gods, is the same term as that applied by the Jews to the spirits that possessed men in the days of the Saviour, and that they reckoned the Gentile gods among those demons. Christ treats them as though they were real possessions. He talks to them, and bids them leave the persons possessed by them. He was talking in the presence of a people who believed in these things, and every look, and word, and act of the Saviour was calculated to confirm them in that belief, whether it was true or false; so that we must infer either the general correctness of this belief, or the intention of Christ to deceive the people.

But the New Testament writers claim that persons possessed of devils were possessed of the spirit of Apollo, the heathen oracle; and that the expulsion of the spirit of Apollo was the casting out of demons.

(Acts xvi, 16, "And it came to pass as we went to prayer, a certain damsel possessed with a spirit of divination met us, which brought her masters much gain by soothsaying. The same followed Paul and us, and cried, saying, These men are the servants of the most high God, which show unto us the way of salvation. And this did she many days. But Paul being grieved, turned and said to the spirit, I command thee in the name of Jesus Christ to come out of her. And he came out the same hour."

This is an important text in the discussion of this subject, as it forms a sort of connecting link between the demoniacal possessions described in the New Testament and the heathen oracles of profane history.

There can be no reasonable doubt that this woman was possessed. Mr. Barnes says, "It is plain that Paul regarded this as a case of demoniacal possession and treated it accordingly." Dr. Clark says, "Had not St.

Luke considered this as a *real case of diabolic possession*, he has made use of the most improper language he could choose; language and forms of speech calculated to deceive all his readers, and cause them to believe a lie."

This woman was "possessed with a spirit of divination," (*pneuma Puthonas.*) Dr. Clarke translates it, "Having a spirit of Python, or of Apollo." This name is not a scriptural name, but like other names found in the Acts of the Apostles, such as Mercury and Jupiter, belongs to the heathen mythology of Greece and Rome, and hence we must turn to the classic writers of those countries for an explanation. Python, or Pythias, was one of the names of Apollo, the Grecian god of the fine arts, of music, poetry, medicine, and eloquence. The temple of this god was at Delphi, as we have seen.

The place where this event occurred (Greece) goes far to identify this instance of inspiration with the other heathen oracles of Greece, particularly the Delphic oracle and its Pythonesses.

"With this historical explanation, we have no difficulty in understanding the circumstances of Paul's miracle in exorcising the woman. As the event did not take place in Delphi, and as the spirit was called, notwithstanding, a spirit of Python, which, according to the Greek idiom, may be as well translated a Pythian spirit, we must conclude that this woman was possessed in exactly the same manner as the Pythoness at Delphi, although she was not connected with that institution."

St. Paul meeting a case of this kind at Ephesus, we are interested to know how he treated it. He commanded the spirit of Apollo to come out of her, the damsel: "And he came out the same hour." If this was not a real possession, we repeat, Paul was the greater juggler of the two. There is not the most distant intimation that there was any difference of opinion between Paul the Jewish

Christian, and the Philippian Greeks interested in this case. Paul, addressing the spirit, said, "Come out of *her*, and *he* came out." When he speaks of the damsel, he uses the feminine *her;* but when he speaks of the spirit, he employs the masculine *he*, clearly showing that they were entirely distinct from each other.

Here we find Paul coming directly in contact with one who was possessed, according to the belief of the Greeks, of the spirit of Apollo; and, according to the belief of the Jews, of the devil, or of a demon. Paul disposes of the case so as to convince the Greeks, or Gentiles, that they were not mistaken as to its being a real possession; and to convince the Jews that they were not mistaken as to the real character of the demon.

Here is the proof that the demons of the New Testament, and the demons that possessed the mediums of Apollo, were one and the same. This text is the connecting link, uniting the sorcery of the ancients with the demonology of the Saviour's day.)

Take the case of Simon Magus, (Acts viii. 9, 10.) He is said to have bewitched the people of Samaria by the use of sorcery.

Sorcerers, we have before seen, are "those who profess to call up the dead;" "those who consult evil spirits." It is, says Webster, "divination by the assistance, or supposed assistance, of evil spirits, or the power of commanding evil spirits." Here is a case similar to the one last named, only there is no evidence that Simon was dispossessed of the demon.

Justin Martyr, speaking of Simon, says:

"After the ascension of our Lord into heaven, certain men were suborned by demons as their agents, who said that they were gods. Simon, a certain Samaritan of the village called Githon, one of the number who, in the reign of Claudius Cesar, performed many magic rites by the operation of demons, was considered a god in the imperial city of Rome, and was honored with a statue as a god. . . . A certain

Helen, also, is of this class, who had before been a public prostitute in Tyre of Phenicia, at that time attached herself to Simon, and was called the first idea that proceeded from him."—*Eusebius*, p. 63.

In this case, as in the one last named, the apostles recognize the existence of demons in those claiming to be inspired by Apollo. This being established, we need not identify the phenomena, as we have clearly shown that ancient sorcery and modern Spiritualism are identical.

We will, however, present a description of a New Testament demon, from the pen of Dr. Olshausen, the German commentator. In his notes on the "Demoniac of Gadara," we find the following description of persons thus possessed:

"In the first place, the condition of the demoniacs appears always to suppose a certain degree of moral delinquency; yet so that their sin manifests itself, not so much in wickedness, properly speaking, as predominant sensuality, (probably lasciviousness in particular,) which was indulged in opposition to their better self. . . . Next, there appears, as a characteristic of demoniacs, a weakening of the bodily organization, particularly the nervous system. . . . But, again, our view is in accordance with the circumstance that, in the descriptions of the demoniacs, we often find a subjection of the nervous system, and with this, of the voluntary bodily functions, especially language, to the will of the demons. They speak their character, or rather the demon speaks through them, but always so that there appears at moments the consciousness of their individuality. This state is quite parallel with the trance, or being in the spirit, and speaking with tongues. And, lastly, we discover also in the demoniacs an enhanced faculty of foreseeing, a kind of somnambulic clairvoyance. . . . At one time they manifest a deep insight into truth; at another, crude popular notions are mixed up in their words, so that their conversation has the fearfully vivid character of the erring and confused talk of madmen, who not unfrequently give utterance to striking thoughts, but so connected with the other elements that the splendor of the thought is only a more melancholy testimony of the greatness of the derangement in the seat of life, whence it issues."

No one can fail to see a correct portrait of Spiritualism here. The reader will do well to consult Olshausen's Notes on Matt. viii, 28–34, covering some fifteen pages of volume one, beginning with page 359.

We think we have now shown that modern Spiritualism is not only Greek and Roman sorcery, but New Testament demonology. There cannot be found one important point in which they differ. This being the case, what is to be thought of this boasted new dispensation of Spiritualism? What is to be thought of intelligent men going back to Greek and Roman idolatry, and uniting with New Testament demons in "What have we to do with thee, Jesus, thou Son of God?" Is it not true, that men "love darkness rather than light?"

CHAPTER IV.

MODERN WITCHCRAFT.

THE witchcraft which prevailed to an alarming extent in Europe during the fifteenth and sixteenth centuries was nothing more than the cropping out of Spiritualism, as we shall be able to show.

If the reader has not taken special pains to investigate the subject, he may be startled by the facts presented, especially the extent to which it prevailed, and its marked likeness to Spiritualism.

WITCHCRAFT ON THE CONTINENT.

During the latter part of the fourteenth century special warrants were from time to time issued in behalf of appointed inquisitors, authorizing them to visit those provinces of Germany, France, and Italy, where any report concerning sorcery had alarmed the public mind; and said commissioners, proud of the trust reposed in them, used their utmost exertion, that the severity of the tortures inflicted might wring the truth from all suspected persons, until they rendered the provinces in which they exercised their jurisdiction a desert from which the inhabitants fled. It would be impossible to credit the extent of the slaughter, had not some of the inquisitors themselves been reporters of their own judicial exploits. The same hand which signed the sentence recorded the execution. (Sir W. Scott.)

As early as 1398, the University of Paris, in laying down rules for the judicial prosecution of witches, expressed regret that the crime was growing more frequent than in any former age.

It is said that the first appearance of sorcery was in Narbonne, in the South of France. It soon reached Paris, Italy, Germany, and finally spread over all the continent.

Pope John XXII. complains bitterly, in 1317, that a number of his courtiers, and even his own physician, had given themselves over to the devil, and had conjured evil spirits into *rings*, *circles*, etc., in order to influence men both at a distance and also near at hand. Ten years later, the same pope complained of the unholy tendency of men toward the magic arts. He says that many have made a compact with hell, and demand of the demons speech and answer. (History of Magic, vol. ii, pp. 153, 154.)

In 1404, a synod was held at Langres, for the purpose of devising means for checking the progress of sorcery.

In 1484, Pope Innocent VIII. issued a bull against the Germans, in which he accuses them of sorcery. He says, "It has come to our ears that numbers of both sexes do not avoid to have intercourse with infernal fiends, and that by their sorceries they afflict both man and beast." The pope expresses his grief that in "Germany, particularly in Upper Germany, Salzburg, and Mainz, Cologne, Trier, and Bremen, many had fallen away from the Catholic faith, and mingled with demons and paramour-devils."

The inquisitors were ordered to "convict, imprison, and punish."

This bull was enforced by the successive bulls of Alexander VI., (1494,) Leo X., (1521,) and Adrian VI., (1522.)

In 1491, Florimond, a Frenchman, wrote a work on antichrist, in which he says, "All those who have offered us some signs of the approach of antichrist agree that the increase of sorcery and witchcraft is to distinguish the melancholy period of his advent; and was ever age afflicted with them as ours? The seats destined for criminals, before our judicatories, are blackened with persons accused of this guilt. There are not judges enough to try them. Our dungeons are gorged with them. No day passes that we do not render our tribunals bloody by the dooms which we pronounce, or in which we do not return to our homes discontented and terrified at the horrible contents of the confessions which it has been our duty to hear. And the devil is accounted so good a master that we cannot commit so great a number of his slaves to the flames but what there shall arise from their ashes a number sufficient to supply their places."—*Sir W. Scott.*

The extent of the executions for sorcery is quite incredible. In Germany alone, not less than one hundred thousand suffered death at the hands of the executioner. Whole provinces are said to have been depopulated, that no sorcerer or witch might escape.

In 1485, large but unknown numbers suffered in Berlin. The same year, one hundred are named who were executed at Piedmont.

In 1488, one thousand were executed at Constance.

In 1515, five hundred were burned at Geneva in three months. During the same year, forty-eight were burned at Ravensburg.

In 1524, one thousand were executed at Como; and one hundred a year for several years afterward.

No less than nine hundred females suffered death at the hands of the executioner at Lorraine.

In 1580, large numbers were executed in Spain.

In 1682, several were executed in Portugal, and eighteen are named who suffered at Avignon.

Sweden was visited about the same time with the dreaded scourge. The king confessed that his "judges and commissioners had caused divers men, women, and children to be burned and executed, on such pregnant evidence as was brought before him."

In France, sorcery had become so common in 1594, that it is said, "The jails were not sufficient to contain the prisoners, nor had they judges enough to try them." Triscala told the king (Charles IX.) that in 1520 there were many thousands in his kingdom.

In 1431, that world-renowned heroine, Joan of Arc, after her wonderful military exploit at the siege of Orleans, was burned for witchcraft, by order of the Earl of Bedford.

Many innocent persons were, without doubt, accused, convicted, and executed. We cannot doubt but the person last named was of this class. Our object is not so much to prove the guilt or innocence of the vast numbers executed for the crime of sorcery or witchcraft, as it is to show the extent to which it prevailed. These facts will give the reader some idea of the extent to which spirit-commerce prevailed on the continent during the fifteenth and sixteenth centuries. The picture is a sad one, but nevertheless true.

SORCERY IN ENGLAND AND SCOTLAND.

The English were sorely afflicted with sorcery. It affected all classes, the ignorant and the learned, the rich and the poor, the high and the low.

Bishop Jewell, in a sermon preached before Queen Elizabeth, in 1558, addresses her thus: "It may please your grace to understand that witches and sorceries, within these last four years, are marvelously increased within your grace's realm. Your subjects pine away even unto death; their color fadeth, their speech is benumbed, their senses are bereft."

The laws of England, down to the fifteenth century, against witches, were as severe as they were on the continent. Afterward simple witchcraft was not punished, except in cases where other crimes were committed in connection with it; in such cases it suffered the full penalty of the law. For instance, the obtaining and circulating pretended prophecies from those possessing *familiar spirits*, if they had a tendency to unsettle the state, or endanger the king's title, were crimes severely punished.

The charge against Edmond Hartley was, "that he had made the magic circle for conjuration." He claimed to be a healing medium.

Not less than thirty thousand persons were executed in England for the crime of sorcery and witchcraft; among the number were the Duke of Buckingham, the Dutchess of Gloucester, the Maid of Kent, Lord Hungerford, and others of like character.

The Scotch were as much afflicted with sorcery as the English were. We are informed, on good authority, that many persons were burned, many transported, and many imprisoned. During a very brief time, it is said, more than four thousand were executed.

In 1563, the following statute, under which all witch trials were subsequently conducted in Scotland, was enacted. The estates enacted that "no person taken upon hand to use any manner of witchcraft, sorcery, or necromancy, nor give themselves forth to have any such craft or knowledge thereof, therethrough abusing the people; that no person seek any help, response, or consultation, or any such uses or abuses of witchcraft, under pain of death."—*Chambers's Domestic Annals of Scotland.*

With regard to the extent of witchcraft in Europe during the time of which we write Dr. Dick says: "Europe was little better than a large suburb or outwork of Pandemonium, one half of the people either bewitching or bewitched."

Dr. Hutchinson says, that "during one century, from 1484, there were more witches executed than had been from the beginning of the world unto then."

The business-like manner in which they executed witches in Scotland may be inferred from the following items, the burning of two witches:

For ten loads of coals to burn them...............	£3	6	8
For a tar barrel................................	0	14	0
For harden to be jumpers for them...............	3	10	0
For making of them............................	0	8	0
For one to go to Finmouth for the laird to sit upon their assize as judge..........................	0	6	0
For the executioner for his pains.................	8	16	0
For his expenses here...........................	0	16	4

We have considered the extent of Spiritualism briefly; let us proceed to examine its phenomena. We believe that the sorcery and witchcraft of the times of which we write were the Spiritualism of our day, and that their identity can be clearly shown.

Whoever reads up the history of those times will be struck with the fact, that females were the most remarkable mediums then, as every one knows them to be now. Historians all agree in this.

Roger Bullingbrook was executed in 1441 for informing the Duchess of Gloucester how long the king would live.

The Maid of Kent, it is said, fell into strange trances, and uttered unusual discourses. The persons who heard her thought her possessed of supernatural power.

The account given by Hutchinson of the conversation between Miss Throgmorton, and Pluck, Hardname, Catch, Blue, and the three Smacks, strikingly reminds us of a modern medium conversing with the spirits of the dead. She falls into a doze, and declares that such a sleep has something of paradise in it. She falls into fits, and strange, unusual postures, etc.

The account given of Meikle John Gibb and his followers, looks to the same relationship. They burn their Bibles in the morelands, as an act of solemn adherence to their new faith. Gibb is transported to America, where he is long venerated by the natives for his familiar converse with the devil. The whole account is but a picture of Spiritualism.

The mediums when in the trance state became insensible to external objects. There were dancing mediums among them, as we find them now. They professed to work miracles. They claimed to foretell future events and cure diseases.

Pordage, an English preacher and physician of Cromwell's time, was a remarkable leader in Spiritualism. He set the inner vision above everything. He established a society, which he named the "Philadelphian Society." There was a large society gathered, finally known as the "Angelic Brethren." Pordage claimed to have intercourse with spirits. They went in and out of his chamber, seen, not only by himself, but by his wife.

In their meetings the members fell into ecstacies, in which they saw visions of heaven and hell, of angels and devils. Such scenes were of daily occurrence in their meetings. They said spirits pass before them, through the outward sight with the inward eye. Evil and good spirits everywhere mixed together.

Jane Lead, a member of Pordage's society, and a very remarkable medium, published a number of volumes, containing revelations from the spirit-land. The titles of some of her works may give the reader some idea of their contents: "Clouds," "The Revelation of Revelations," "The Laws of Paradise," "An Embassy to the Philadelphian Society," etc.

A daughter of a Protestant clergyman is said to have had visions, transports, and communion with spirits, with her eyes open and closed, by night and by day. Such were the wonderful visions seen, and prophecies uttered, that Bohemia and Germany were kept in a state of excitement for a long time.

Peter Apon, of Padua, claimed to have been taught the seven learned arts by spirits from the spirit-world.

The blind conjuror of Paris pretended to deal only with good angels.

The Surrey demoniac was simply a dancing

medium. He said he had given his soul to the devil, that he might be the best dancer in Lancashire. He could talk Latin, though ignorant of the language. He was able to relate matters at a distance of which he had no knowledge. He was accustomed to go to a certain place to converse with a spirit.

The devils are said to have played all kinds of beautiful pieces of music on the harp. (History of Magic, vol. ii, p. 180.)

The nuns of Loudun, who are reported as doing so many wonders, such as speaking languages, revealing secrets, writing miraculously, etc., were simply spiritualistic mediums.

Agnes Sympson, in 1599, confessed to King James that she was a healing medium.

Nostrodamus, a French physician, was the author of a large book of prophecies, the productions professedly of spirits.

In 1576, Bessie Dunlop, of Dalry, was accused of sorcery, witchcraft, and abuse of the people. She professed to tell of coming illness, and where lost goods could be found.

Her judges inquired of her by what art she could make such disclosures. Now mark her reply. She said, of herself, she had no knowledge or science of such matters, but that when questioned concerning such matters she was in the habit of applying to one Thomas Reid, who had been killed at the battle of Pinkie, November 10, 1547, as he himself affirmed, and that he resolved her any questions which she asked him.

She seems to have been a seeing medium, as she described his general appearance and dress with great minuteness.

Her first interview with Reid was at a season of deep affliction. He informed her where stolen goods could be found. He also informed her what remedies to administer to the sick. Many remarkable cases of cure are reported, under Reid's directions, all going to prove that she was a seeing and healing medium, equal to those of our day, who claim to be in communication with the spirits of the dead.

Alison Pearson, of Byrehill, was executed in

1588 for invoking the spirit of the devil in the person of one William Sympson, her cousin, who she affirmed was a great doctor of medicine. He taught her what remedies to use, and how to apply them.

So much confidence had the people in her skill to heal, that the Archbishop of St. Andrews, created by James VI., actually took her prescriptions and was cured.

This medium is said to have had continual visions, both sleeping and waking. In these visions she claimed to be associated with the queen of the elves, or spirits.

Need we say more to convince the candid reader that here is a full length portrait of modern spiritualism? It is the same in its mediums and phenomena. Hence the oft-repeated declaration of spiritualists, that its present development is something new under the sun, and Judge Edmonds's "New Dispensation," etc., is proved baseless. It is the old dispensation of hell not yet abrogated.

Our authorities agree in fixing the time of

its chief prevalence, namely, during the fifteenth and sixteenth centuries.

The reader will remember the testimony of the University of Paris, that in 1398 the crime was growing more frequent than in any former age; also the statement of Florimond, that in 1491 no age was so much afflicted as that. Then, in 1691, Rev. Robert Kirk, a Scottish minister of the Highlands, wrote a book, in which he describes the acts of demons, who possessed persons in his day, he says, to some extent, but more in the past. By these facts we see that it prevailed generally, in connection with the Reformation under Luther, and most extensively in Germany, where Luther labored. This I regard as a significant fact in the history of this strange movement.

What is there in modern Spiritualism not found in the sorcery and witchcraft of the fifteenth and sixteenth centuries?

Does Spiritualism boast of a multiplicity of mediums? They could boast of the cursing medium, and the blessing medium; of the medium of art, and the medium of compact; the active medium, and the passive medium; the developed medium, and the undeveloped medium.

Does Spiritualism boast of seeing mediums? So could they.

Does Spiritualism boast of healing mediums? They could point you to the cures effected.

Does Spiritualism boast of speaking mediums? They could speak as fluently.

Does Spiritualism boast of writing mediums? They could also point you to numerous volumes dictated, professedly, by the spirits of the unseen world.

Does Spiritualism boast of musical mediums? They could sing and play as sweetly.

Does Spiritualism boast of dancing mediums? So could they.

Does Spiritualism arrogate to itself prophetic power? They claimed the same.

Does Spiritualism claim to be able to accurate ly describe events transpiring at a distance They did the same.

Finally, Does Spiritualism claim to be in constant communication with the spirit-world? This was also their constant boast.

Tell me, then, is not the Spiritualism of the nineteenth, the sorcery and witchcraft of the fifteenth and sixteenth centuries? Are they not members of the same family? Have they not all one father?

Spiritualists would have us believe that the marshaled hosts of the unseen world are invading our earth for the first time.

"Spiritualism," says the "Banner of Light," January 18, 1862, "is the dawn of a new era, to be marked by a complete and radical change in all things; to introduce a new condition of society upon the earth, with a new religion, a new state, and a new order of men and women. As such, we should announce and disseminate it."

But we have shown that Spiritualism was more rampant and widespread during the fifteenth and sixteenth centuries than in our day. It is only the resurrection of the old witchcraft of the past, upon which the verdict of the ages has been pronounced.

For the sake of morality, intelligence, and the honor of humanity, let not that corrupt and ignoble form be exhumed from its sleep of ages; for in the plain old Saxon of the Bible, "by this time it stinketh."

CHAPTER V.

SALEM WITCHCRAFT.

THAT diabolical influence which swept over Europe, producing terrible havoc among all classes, resulting in the death of hundreds of thousands of human beings, made its appearance in New England about the latter part of the seventeenth century, under the well known name of "Salem Witchcraft."

We have been inclined to laugh at the ghostly credulity of the authorities of Salem. But after giving the history of that period a careful perusal, I confess I have no disposition to make myself merry at their expense. Few persons who have not taken special pains to investigate that chapter in the history of New England, have a just conception of its real character.

Dr. Bently, in his "History of Salem," says,

"From March to August, 1692, was the most distressing time Salem ever knew; business was interrupted, the town was deserted, terror was in every countenance, and distress in every heart. Fear haunted every street, melancholy dwelt in silence in every place after the sun retired."

Judge Story, in a discourse delivered at Salem, September 18th, 1828, says: "But surely our ancestors had no special reasons for shame in a belief which had the universal sanction of our own and former ages, which counted in its train philosophers as well as enthusiasts, which was graced by the learning of prelates as well as by the countenance of kings; which the law supported by its mandates, and the purest judges felt no compunctions in enforcing."

But it must be remembered that Salem was not the first place in which it made its appearance in New England. Some time before 1692 men and women were condemned and executed for the crime of witchcraft in various towns in New England. Margaret Jones was executed for this crime in Charlestown, Mass., in 1648. A woman in Dorchester, another in Cambridge, and another in Boston, were executed for the same crime. Some time after this, two or three were executed in Springfield, and one in Hartford. These were all executed before 1665. Between this last period and 1689, Mr. and Mrs. Greenwood, Mary Johnson, and Miss Gover, of Boston, were executed.

These cases of condemnation and execution had prepared the public mind for the wonderful outbreak at Salem, which occurred in 1692, and which filled many a New England home with sorrow. It manifested itself in Salem, in February, 1692, in the family of Rev. Mr. Parris, the settled minister of the town. His daughter Elizabeth, about nine, and his niece, Abigail Williams, about twelve years old, and Ann Putnam, a young female in the town, were the first to be afflicted. Such was their conduct as to induce physicians to pronounce them bewitched.

Sarah Good, Sarah Osborn, and Tituba, an

Indian woman residing in Mr. Parris's family, were supposed to be the witches. These persons were supposed to have made an actual, deliberate and formal compact with the devil, to become his faithful subjects and do what they could to promote his cause. They were supposed to be capable of doing anything that the devil could do. An almost indefinite amount of supernatural ability was supposed to result from this diabolical compact. From this simple beginning it spread with fearful rapidity over all New England. On the 11th of March, Mr. Parris invited several ministers in the neighborhood to unite with him in holding a solemn fast at his house, that by prayer to God the evil might be removed from his family. Tituba, Mr. Parris's Indian woman, was complained of first, as being a witch.

A court, consisting of seven judges, was formed for trying the accused. Their names were: Lieutenant-Governor Stoughton, Major Saltonstall, Major Richards, Major Gidny, Mr. Wait Winthrop, Capt. Sewall, and Mr. Sargeant. Their first meeting was at the court-house in Salem, June 2, 1692.

There were presented before this honorable court about two hundred persons accused of the crime of witchcraft. Fifty-five escaped death by confessing the crime; one hundred and fifty were imprisoned, twenty were executed, and eight others were condemned to death, but subsequently released.

The names and residence of the accused, and the date and manner of their death, (all occurring in the year 1692,) are as follows:

Bridget Bishop, of Salem, hanged, June 10th; Sarah Good and Rebecca Nurse, of Salem, Susanna Martin, of Amesbury, Elizabeth How, of Ipswich, and Sarah Wilder, of Topsfield, were hanged July 10th; Rev. George Burroughs, of Wells, Maine, and former minister of Salem, John Proctor, John Willard, and George Jacobs, Sen., of Salem, and Martha Carrier, of Andover, were hanged August 19th; Giles Cory, of Salem, refusing to be put upon his trial, and pleading "not guilty" to the indictment, was pressed to death, September 16th; Martha Cory, Alice Parker, and Ann Pudeater, of Salem, Mary Easty, of Topsfield, Margaret Scott, of Rowley, William Reed, of Marblehead, Samuel Wardwell and Mary Parker, of Andover, were hanged September 22d. Here ended the execution of witches in Salem and New England.

That a very marked reaction should have taken place, after such an intense excitement and unjustifiable sacrifice of life, for causes which they did not seem to understand, was very natural. The judges made a long and humble confession of injustice done the accused. They implored pardon of the surviving sufferers, and of God, through Jesus Christ, that they might be accepted and the land saved from the curse which their sins merited. One stands up in a Boston meeting-house while his confession is being read. He earnestly solicits the prayers of the people of God for himself, his family, and a land in mourning. The minister of Salem, Rev. Mr. Parris, confesses his error.

But the good people will no longer consent to listen to his ministrations, and he is obliged to retire.

Men who had little faith in spiritual things, began to write and publish refutations of the witch mania. They took, generally, the opposite extreme. Robert Calef, a merchant in Boston, published a work on the subject, entitled, "More Wonders of the Invisible World," which Cotton Mather calls a "vile volume," and Dr. Increase Mather, then president of Harvard College, ordered to be burnt in the college-yard, as a "wicked book." It must be confessed that Mr. Calef's book is a little one-sided on the subject, and was evidently intended to deal a heavier blow against the Mathers than against witchcraft. It is claimed that Hutchinson, in his "History of Witchcraft," speaks with favor of Mr. Calef's work. But it must be remembered that Mr. Hutchinson took the same view of witchcraft that Mr. Calef did, and it is not strange that he should have been prejudiced in his favor.

We cannot dwell longer on the mere *history* of this matter. We come, more especially, to consider its phenomena. We shall find, on a close examination of these, all or nearly all the phenomena of modern Spiritualism.

The persons who are said to have been afflicted were horribly distorted and convulsed. Marks of violence were found upon their persons. Their hands were tied close together with cords and they lifted from the earth in the presence of a crowd of people. An iron spindle was wrested from a demon and secured by lock and key, and subsequently removed by the demon. Good, credible people, gave oath that they saw the corner of a sheet torn from a specter or demon, by a person assaulted, and that a man had his hand nearly wrung off by a demon, in an attempt to get possession of it. Money was taken by demons and then dropped from the air into the hands of the afflicted.

Of Ann Cole, of Hartford, it is reported that when under the influence of demons, "her tongue was improved to express things unknown to herself. Several eminent ministers wrote the speeches of the spirits, thus heard in the mouth of this Ann Cole."—*Magnalia*, vol. ii, p. 390. Elizabeth Knap was so under the influence of demons that she knew not what she said, and she spoke against godly persons, even against her will. Her speech was very remarkable.

The house of William Morse, of Newberry, seems as remarkable for spirit manifestations as the Fox house at Hydeville. Bricks, sticks, and stones were frequently thrown at the house. Pieces of wood moved by an unseen hand. A long staff danced up and down the chimney, and it was as much as two persons could do to hold it. An iron crook was violently hurled about by an invisible hand. A chair flew about the room and lit upon the table. A chest was carried from one place in the house to another. Keys flew about the house. What resembled a large stone would be thrown upon the bed at night. A box, a board, and a bag of hops were thrown upon the bed. The man of the house was knocked down by an unseen hand. An ink-horn was violently snatched away, and afterwards dropped from the air. A cap was pulled from the head of one. A lady going down cellar, the trap-door was immediately closed after her, and for some time secured against her egress. Bed-clothes were pulled from the bed and the bed shaken; chairs danced about the room, and what seemed to be a human hand was felt upon members of the family. A distinct rapping was heard on the bedstead, on boards, etc.

These are only a few of the things which happened to this family.

The house of Mr. G. Walton, of Portsmouth, was visited with similar phenomena. It is said that stones were thrown at and around the house. Many articles were hurled about the rooms. Stones would even fly upon the table. A spit was carried up the chimney and returned, and on being touched flew out of the window. Mr. Philip Smith, of Hadley, was most wonderfully affected. Knockings were heard about his bed at night. He spoke with great fluency, and in several languages of which he had no knowledge.

The children of John Goodwin, who were thought to have been bewitched by Miss Gover, of Boston, performed feats of a remarkable character. They would pass for some distance through the air, as though they were flying. They told of some silver plate in a well, of which they had no natural means of knowing. They could understand conversation in Latin, Greek, and Hebrew, of which languages they had no knowledge. One of these girls paraphrased the 31st Psalm in strains that perfectly amazed those who listened to her. She also foretold the horrible Indian tragedies that would be enacted in the land, etc. (Magnalia, vol. ii, p. 398.)

The witches, as they were called, would cry out much against godly men and women. Those who were the most fluent are said to have been the most wicked. "They said they knew not what, but were in a preternatural dream." (Magnalia.)

Persons afflicted could tell of the approach of their tormentors, when their eyes were closed. They were stiff and rigid. Calef reports one person who was drawn up to the ceiling. (Letter I, § 8.) How perfectly does this harmonize with the facts of Spiritualism!

President Mahan says, "Rev. H. Snow, in his work entitled 'Spirit Intercourse,' gives an apparently well-authenticated case, in which a medium was himself 'raised entirely from the floor, and held in a suspended position by the same kind of invisible power.' For ourselves, we have no disposition to question such a statement, knowing as we do, that cases perfectly similar and analogous are attested by evidence which we are compelled to regard as valid."—*Mod. Mys.*, p. 117.

(In a letter written Oct. 8, 1692, by Thomas Brattle, F.R.S., on the subject of the "Salem Witchcrafts," and published in the "Collection of the Mass. Hist. Society," (1st Series, vol. 5,) the author administers a severe rebuke to the "Salem gentlemen," as he calls them, for the manner in which they condemned and executed persons for alleged witchcraft; giving it as his opinion, which I think a correct one, that the persons who professed to be bewitched were the persons who were in league with the devil, and not the persons accused by them. He says, "I think the matter might be better solved another way; but I shall not make any attempt that way, further than to say that these afflicted children, as they are called, do hold correspondence with the devil even in the esteem and account of the S. G., [Salem gentlemen,] for when the black man, the devil, does appear to them, they ask him many questions, and accordingly give information to the inquirer; and if this is not holding correspondence with the devil, I know not what is." P. 64.

This writer further states, that many persons brought their sick friends and relatives to these afflicted children, to learn the nature of the disease with which they were afflicted, not because of any ordinary knowledge they might possess, but because of "a supernatural knowledge; a knowledge which they obtain by their holding correspondence with specters, or evil spirits, as they themselves grant. This consulting of these afflicted children, as above said, seems to me to be a very gross evil, a real abomination, not fit to be known in New England, and yet is a thing practiced, not only by Tom and John—I mean the ruder and more ignorant sort—but by many who profess high, and pass among us for some of the better sort." P. 70. He further declares that some of the "civil leaders and spiritual teachers allow of, encourage, yea, and practice this very abomination." A person went from Boston to Salem to consult these persons with regard to his sick child, and did so; for which he was severely reproved by Rev. Increase Mather. The doctor wished to know "whether there was not a God in Boston, that he should go to the devil in Salem for advice."

Mr. Brattle says, "This consulting of these afflicted children about their sick, was the unhappy beginning of the unhappy troubles at poor Andover." P. 71.

"The afflicted do own and assert," says Mr. Brattle, "and the justices do grant, that the devil does inform and tell the afflicted the names of those persons that are thus unknown unto them." He further says, "It is most certain that it is neither Almighty God, nor yet any good spirit that gives this information; and my reason is good—because God is a God of truth, and the good spirits will not lie; whereas these informations have several times proved false, when the accused were brought before the afflicted." P. 73.

Here are some of the facts of the New England witchcraft. They are very remarkable, and certainly very well authenticated. Cotton Mather says, and he was no mean man, and has never been accused of dishonesty, "Flashy people may burlesque these things; but when hundreds of the most sober people, in a country where they have as much mother-wit certainly as the rest of mankind, know them to be true, nothing but the absurd and froward spirit of Sadduceism can question them. I have not yet mentioned so much as one thing that will not be justified, if it be required, by the oaths of more considerate persons than any that can ridicule these odd phenomena."—*Magnalia*, vol. i, p. 187.

Mr. Thatcher makes a lame effort to disprove these facts. His work, on the whole, is a lame affair. It opens with a chapter on "Ghosts," and concludes with one on "Quackery;" and his book should have been entitled "Ghostly Quackery."

Dr. Hutchinson, in reviewing this history, gives a false coloring to the whole matter, and suppresses some of the most prominent facts. Dr. Samson, in his recent work, "Spiritualism Tested," gives most of the facts, but attempts to account for them on natural principles. In order to make good his theory, he represents Rev. George Burroughs as a burly, muscular, portly, gigantic Englishman; and Cotton Mather a slender, delicate, nervous, thoughtful, reflective, impulsive student. But if Dr. Samson's theory rests on the portly, gigantic Burroughs, it must have a frail foundation, for he is said by

Mather to have been a "puny man," and by Calef, a "small, black-haired man." How Dr. Samson could have magnified this puny, small, black-haired Burroughs into a burly, portly, gigantic Englishman, is a little difficult for us to understand. But anything to make good the theory.

We have thus presented a very brief history of Salem or New England witchcraft; and in glancing at its phenomena, we have met with all the peculiar characteristics of our modern Spiritualism.

Do spiritualists claim to have intercourse with spirits? So did they.

Do spiritualists claim to reveal future events? So did they.

Do spiritualists claim to move tables, and turn up things generally? So did they.

Do spiritualists claim to pronounce wonderful discourses by the aid of invisible spirits? So did they.

Do spiritualists claim to produce rappings by the aid of unseen agents? So did they.

Do spiritualists profess to speak in an unknown tongue? So did they.

Do spiritualists profess to heal the sick by prescriptions from the spirit world? So did they.

Do spiritualists claim to be the opponents of the Christian religion? So did they.

Do spiritualists proclaim against the Bible? So did they.

Stripped of all the foolish notions peculiar to that age, New England witchcraft stands before us the younger brother of ancient demonology, and the elder brother of modern Spiritualism.

CHAPTER VI.

THE SPIRIT OF MASCON AND THE EPWORTH RAPPINGS.

I PROPOSE giving in this chapter two very marked and well-attested developments of Spiritualism; one occurring in Mascon, Burgundy, and the other in Epworth, England. The latter of these accounts is familiar to many; the former, though equally well attested, is not so generally known. It is entitled, "A True Relation of the Chief Things which an Evil Spirit did and said at Mascon in Burgundy." The wonderful things here narrated occurred in the house of Rev. Mr. Perreaud, minister of the Reformed Church in Mascon. He seems tc have been a very pious and intelligent man. "The pastors and elders of the Reformed Churches of the province of Burgundy, assembled in a synod at Bussy, in the balliage of

Chalons-upon-Stone, certify to all, that Mr. Perreaud, minister of the Gospel, exercised the charge of the holy ministry in this province for the space of fifty years; first in his own town of Bussy, where he was born, being descended of the most ancient family of the town, and since in the Church of Mascon, and afterward in the Churches of the balliage of Gez: in all that time, and in all these Churches doing the office of a good pastor and a faithful servant of God, both in doctrine and life; of which he had an especial testimonial given him by the Church of Mascon in the year 1649, the said Church expressing much satisfaction of his godliness and singular charity." They further add, that, "it hath pleased God to bring him into many, and some very extraordinary trials, especially while he served the Church of Mascon, yet the same God hath strengthened him with constant health of body and godly tranquillity of mind, and hath endued him with virtue to bear and overcome all his afflictions," etc.

The account will be given in an abridged

form from a translation made by Peter du Molin, at the request of Sir Robert Boyle, and chiefly in the language of Mr. Perreaud.

Mr. Perreaud informs us that on the 14th of September, 1612, he went to Couches, with one of the elders of the Church of Mascon, to attend a meeting, and was absent five days. On his return he found his wife and maid in a very great consternation, apparent in their countenance. He asked the cause of it. His wife informed him that the night after he went from town, being in bed and asleep, she was aroused by something which drew her curtain with great noise and violence. The maid, sleeping in the same room, being aroused by the noise, hastily ran to her mistress to inquire the cause. All being quiet, she retired. The next night the maid occupied the same bed with her mistress. No sooner were they comfortably in bed than they felt something draw off the blankets. The maid, attempting to go out of the room, found the door bolted both within and without. She called a young man in another room, who arose and opened the door. Lighting a candle, she found the pewter and brass thrown about the kitchen. The next night the spirit made a great noise among the pewter and brass; also, a noise resembling the hiving of bees.

Mr. Perreaud hearing these relations was not a little amazed; yet he resolved that he would not be too credulous, nor yet too incredulous. "Wherefore," he says, "before I went to bed I carefully searched all the corners of the house, and set bolts and barricadoes to all the doors and windows, stopping even the very cat-holes, leaving nothing that might occasion suspicion of imposture; and after I had prayed with my family I went to bed, while my wife and maid sat spinning by the fire, with a lamp burning on the table.

"I had scarcely got in bed before I heard a great noise in the kitchen, as the rolling of a billet thrown with great strength. I heard also a knocking against a partition of wainscot (that is, walls made in panels) in the same kitchen;

sometimes as with the point of the fingers; sometimes as with the nails; sometimes as with the fist, and then the blows did redouble. Many things were thrown against the wainscot, such as plates, trenchers, and ladles; music was made with a brass colander," etc. Mr. Perreaud, after listening to these noises for some time, arose and went into the room from which they proceeded, the maid holding the light, and searched narrowly that he might find some one hidden in the room. This he did twice, but finding no one, returned to his bed. "Then did I know," he says, "that all this could not proceed but from a wicked spirit."

The next day Mr. Perreaud informed the elders of his Church, and some other worthy men of the town, of the strange occurrences at his house. They subsequently visited his house every evening during the continuance of the noises.

On the 20th of September, in the presence of many witnesses, the spirit appeared, and three or four times whistled with a very loud and shrill tone. It soon framed an articulate voice, and in a hoarse tone pronounced these words, "Two and twenty pence," in a little tune of five notes, which whistling birds were taught to sing. It then pronounced the word "minister" many times. Mr. Perreaud replied, "Get thee from me, Satan; the Lord rebuke thee." The spirit would repeat the Lord's prayer, the creed, the ten commandments, and even sing the eighty-first Psalm. It informed Mr. Perreaud that his father had been poisoned, and gave the place, time, and manner in which it was done. Mr. Perreaud says:

"That very night he said he came from Pais de Vaux; that he had passed through the village of Allagmone, at the door of my eldest brother's house, where he had seen him, with M. du Pan, Minister of Thoiry; that they were ready to go to supper together at my brother's house. He had saluted them, and asked whether they had anything to command him to deliver to me, because he was going to Mascon."

Mr. Perreaud states that he had been informed by Mr. Du Pan, that at the very time he remembered that a man on horseback had spoken with them, and such discourse had passed between them. The demon also informed them of a company that came near being drowned, and that Mr. Perreaud's brother was of the number. Many other things of like character are reported in the account given, and acknowledged by the parties. The demon spoke of the intention of Mr. Perreaud's brother to visit him on a given occasion, and the cause of the change in his mind. Also, of a quarrel between James Berard and Samuel du Mont, which nearly resulted in Berard's death. Particulars of the quarrel were given, which had not been known, but which proved to be true.

"Another night," says Mr. Perreaud, "the demon speaking to one of our company, told him such secret things that the man who affirmed never to have told them to any person, came to believe that the devil knew his thoughts."

"Then he began to mock God and all religion." The dog of the house, which used to bark at all noises, was never known to bark during these disturbances.

The demon proposed to make his will, and wished them to send for a royal notary. He then denied that he was the same person or demon who had spoken to them before. He sung many profane songs, and counterfeited the voice of mountebanks, and especially the huntsmen's cry, "*Ho levrier.*"

Speaking of those who professed the Reformed religion within the kingdom of France, he made this exclamation, 'O, poor Huguenots! you shall have much to suffer within a few years! O, what mischief is intended against you!'"

Mr. Perreaud says, "As his words were strange, so were his actions; for besides those things already related, he did many more of the same kind. He frequently tossed about a great roll of cloth of fifty ells, which a friend had left at my house. Once he snatched a brass candlestick out of the maid's hand, leaving the candle lighted in her hand. He would often take the maid's coats and hang them over the bedposts. Sometimes he would hang at those posts a great starching plate, with cords tied with such a number of knots, that it was impossible to unloose them, and yet himself would untie them in a moment," etc.

"One afternoon a friend of mine visited me. We went together into the chamber where the demon was most resident. There we found the featherbed, blankets, sheets, and bolster, laid on the floor. I called the maid to make the bed, which she did in our presence. But frequently, while we were walking in the same room, we saw the bed tumbled down on the floor as it was before.

"In my study, I found several times part of my books laid on the floor."

"We heard," says Mr. Perreaud, "for a long time, a harmony not unpleasant, of two bells tied together. These were heard in other houses in the town.

His last acts were, throwing stones about the house. A stone was one day thrown at Mr.

Tornus, who took it up and marked it with a coal, and threw it back again. The stone was soon thrown back again, known by the coal mark on it. Mr. Tornus taking it up found it to be hot, and remarked that he believed it had been in hell since he handled it last.

These are the facts, or a few of the facts connected with this strange affair. The Bishop of Mascon hearing the reports, sent for Mr. Tornus to know the truth. He sent also his own secretary, Mr. Chamber, to Mr. Perreaud, to learn the particulars from his own lips. "These two gentlemen, Tornus and Chamber, have told me since," says Mr. Perrault, "that the bishop had heard that story with great admiration, and had some records of the same."

Mr. Wesley published this account in the "Arminian Magazine," in 1782, prefaced with this remark:

"I do not think any unprejudiced men can doubt the truth of this narrative. The truth of it was in the last century acknowledged by all Europe; against which the unaccountableness of it is no objection to those who are convinced of the littleness of their own knowledge."

The famous Robert Boyle, while residing at Geneva, became acquainted with Mr. Perreaud, and received from him the book from which this account is taken, written in French.

In the following note to Rev. Peter du Molin, chaplain to Charles II., and prebendary of Canterbury, requesting its translation into English, he says:

"To the Rev. and Learned Friend, Dr. Peter du Molin:

"Dear Sir:—Though I suppose you will look upon my sending you Monsieur Perreaud's French book as a minding you of the promise you were the other day pleased to make me of putting it into an English dress, yet I hope you will do me the right to believe that if the subject were not extraordinary, I should think it injurious to the public and to you, to be accessory to your turning translator of another's books, that hath already manifested, in several languages, how able you are to write excellent ones of your own.

"I must freely confess to you, that the powerful inclinations which my course of life and studies hath given me to backwardness of assent, and the many fictions which are wont to blemish the relation where spirits and witches are concerned, would make me very backward to contribute anything to your publishing, or any man's believing, a story less strange than this of Monsieur Perreaud.

"But the conversation I had with that pious author during my stay at Geneva, and the present he was pleased to make me of this treatise before it was printed, in a place where I had opportunities to inquire both after the writer and some passages of the book, did at length overcome in me (as to this narrative) all my settled indisposedness to believe strange things. And since I find that you have received an account both of Monsieur Perreaud himself, and several things relating to this book, from that excellent person, your father, I have no reason to doubt but that your skill in the tongues will bring it the greatest advantages that it can receive from a translator's pen. So the reputation which your and your learned father's name will give it, will prove as effectual as anything of that nature can be, to make wary readers believe even the amazing passages of it.

"I am, sir, your affectionate friend and humble servant, ROBERT BOYLE."

The reply to the foregoing, accompanying the translation, is somewhat lengthy. I shall insert a part of it only.

"TO THE HONORABLE AND MOST EMINENT IN GOODNESS AND LEARNING, MR. ROBERT BOYLE:

"SIR,—In obedience to the charge which you have been pleased to lay upon me, I have translated this admirable story, worthy to be known of all men. . . . Many relations are extant of manifestations of demons; the most certain are the history of the Gospel, how the devils spake aloud out of possessed bodies in the presence of great multitudes. . . . But no history relates such a public, continued, and undeniable manifestation of the wicked spirit as this does. . . . For this conversation of the devil was not in a corner, or in a desert, but in the midst of a great city, in a house where there was daily a great consort to hear him speak, and where men of contrary religions met together; whose proneness to cast a disgrace upon the dissenting parties did occasion the examining and the full confirming of the truth thereof, both by the magistrates and by the diocesan of the place. All these particulars and many more have been related to my father, when he was president of a national synod in those parts, by the man that was most concerned in them, the author of this book, a religious, well poised, and venerable divine, who, (if he be still alive,) is above eighty years of age. He wrote this relation when it was fresh in his memory; yet did not publish it till forty-one years after, in the year 1653, being compelled to it by the various and false relations of that story which were scattered abroad. . . . But yourself, sir, had from the author a more immediate information, which being prefixed before this narrative, gives it a free and uncontrollable pass to be admitted into the belief of the most severe and judicious readers. Neither will they have a less opinion of the utility than truth of this relation, when they see that a person so high in learning, so deep in judgment, so real in godliness, so exemplary in good works, hath judged it to be of principal use for the convincing of unbelievers, and the confirming of those that are in the faith. Thereby also I shall reap this benefit to myself, that the world shall know I am honored with your commands, and that I delight to approve myself, sir, your most humble and obedient servant and true honorer,

PETER DU MOLIN."

In this account we find many of the developments of modern Spiritualism—speaking, rapping, music, disarranging furniture, throwing articles about the house, accurately describing events at a distance unknown to the parties present at the time, etc.

The next exhibition of Spiritualism, to which we call the reader's attention, is known as the

EPWORTH RAPPINGS.

These rappings, as they are called, occurred in 1716, in the house of Rev. Samuel Wesley, Rector of Epworth parish, England, and father of John and Charles Wesley, founders of the Methodist denomination. They have occasioned no little discussion and speculation for the last hundred and forty-five years. They were on this wise.

On the night of Dec. 2, 1716, Mr. Wesley's servant, Robert Brown, and one of the maids of the family, were alone in the dining-room. About ten o'clock they heard a strong knocking on the outside of the door which opened into the garden. They at once responded to the call by opening the door, but found no one there. A second knock was heard, accompanied by a groan. The door was again and again opened, as the knocks were repeated, but seeing nothing, and being a little startled, they quietly retired for the night. On Robert reaching the top of the stairs, a hand-mill at a little distance was seen to whirl about with great rapidity. On beholding the strange sight, he seemed only to regret that it had not been full of malt. Strange noises were heard in and about his room during the night. These were related to another maid in the morning only to receive a hearty laugh, and, "What a couple of fools are you!"

This was the simple beginning of the "Epworth Rappings." We shall not attempt to give them in detail, but merely present some of the more important phenomena bearing upon our subject.

Some of the things said to have occurred are the following: Knockings were heard on the doors, on the bedsteads, and at various times in every part of the house by night and by day. Mr. Wesley says that his daughters, Susanna and Ann. were one evening below stairs, in the dining-room, and while there heard a knocking, first at the door, then over their heads. The night after they heard similar knockings under their feet, though no person was in the chamber in the one case, nor below them in the other. He adds, "The like they and my servants heard in both the kitchens, at the door against the partition and over them." Again, "knocking at the foot of the bed and behind it." "We heard several loud knocks in our own chamber, on my side of the bed." The 21st. "That night I was waked a little before one by nine distinct very loud knocks, which seemed to be in the next room to ours, with a sort of a pause at every third stroke." "The next night I heard six knocks." Emily heard the knocks on the bedstead, and under the bed. "She knocked and it answered her." Dec. 26th, when in the nursery, "it began with knocking in the kitchen underneath, then it seemed to be at the bed's feet, then under the bed; at last at the head of it. I went down stairs," says Mr. Wesley, "and knocked with my stick against the joists of the kitchen. It answered me as often and as loud as I knocked." Knockings were heard under the table, etc.

Latches of doors would move up and down as the members of the family approached them. The doors were violently thrust against those who attempted to open and shut them. A cradle was heard to violently rock, where no cradle had been for years. At evening prayer, when the rector "began the prayer for the king, a knocking began all round the room, and a thundering knock attended the amen." This was repeated morning and evening while prayer for the king was being offered. Mr. Wesley says, "I have been thrice pushed by an invisible power, once against the corner of my desk in the study, a second time against the door of the matted chamber, a third time against the right side of the frame of my study door, as I was going in."

Mr. Hoole, vicar of Haxey, an eminently pious and sensible man, was sent for to spend a few evenings with the family. The knockings commenced about ten o'clock in the evening. Mr. Wesley and his friend went into the nursery, where the knockings were heard, and found them to proceed from the head of the bed in which the children were sleeping. Mr. Wesley observed that the children, though asleep, were very much affected; they trembled exceedingly and sweat profusely; and becoming very angry, he pulled out a pistol, and was about to fire at the place from whence the sound came. Mr. Hoole caught him by the arm, and said, "Sir, you are convinced this is something preternatural. If so you cannot hurt it; but you give it power to hurt you." Then going close to the place, Mr. Wesley said sternly, "Thou deaf and dumb devil, why dost thou fright these children, that cannot answer for themselves? Come to me in my study, that am a man." Instantly it knocked the rector's knock, (a particular knock which he always used at the gate,) as if it would shiver the board in pieces." Nothing more was heard that night. Up to this time there had been no noises heard in the study. "But the next evening, as he attempted to go into his study, (of which none had any key but himself,) when he opened the door it was thrust back with such violence as had like to have thrown him down. Presently there was knocking, first on one side, then on the other."

A sound was heard as if a large iron bell were thrown among bottles under the stairs. As Mr. and Mrs. Wesley were going down the broad stairs, they heard a sound as if a vessel of silver were poured upon Mrs. Wesley's breast, and ran jingling down to her feet; at another time, as if all the pewter was thrown about the kitchen, though on examination all was found undisturbed.

The dog, a large mastiff, seemed as much disturbed by these noises as the family. On their approach he would run to Mr. and Mrs. Wesley, seeking shelter between them. "While the disturbances continued he used to bark and leap, and snap on one side and the other, and that frequently before any person in the room heard any noise at all. But after two or three days he used to tremble, and creep away before the noise began. And by this the family knew it was at hand; nor did the observation ever fail." Footsteps were heard in every part of the house, which shook it from cellar to garret. Groans were repeatedly heard, as from a person dying; and at other times it would "sweep through the halls and along the stairs with a sound of a person trailing a loose gown on the floor, and the chamber walls meanwhile shook with vibrations." It frequently responded to Mrs. Wesley if she stamped on the floor and bade it answer. Whenever it was attributed to rats the noises became more loud and fierce.

Susannah Wesley says: "To my father's no small amazement, his trencher [a wooden plate] danced upon the table a pretty while, without any body stirring the table."

These disturbances continued for some months and then subsided, except that some members of the family were annoyed by them, more or less, for some years.

Mr. Wesley was repeatedly urged to quit the

house, but his reply was characteristic: "No, let the devil flee from me; I will never flee from the devil."

Every effort was made to discover the cause of these strange phenomena, but without any satisfactory result, save that all believed them to be preternatural, and the work of the devil. The whole Wesley family were unanimous in this belief.

Dr. Priestley confessed it to have been "the best authenticated and best told story of the kind that is anywhere extant; and yet such were his materialistic views and feelings that he could not find for it what might seem to be a common-sense explanation. He thinks it quite probable that it "was a trick of the servants, assisted by some of the neighbors, and that nothing was meant by it besides puzzling the family and amusing themselves." But Mrs. Wesley and other members of the family state that the noises were heard above and beneath them, when all the family were in the same room.

Mr. Southey, though he does not express an opinion in his Life of Wesley with regard to these noises, does say, "The testimony upon which it rests is far too strong to be set aside because of the strangeness of the relation." He subsequently, in a letter to Mr. Wilberforce, avows his belief in their preternatural character.

Dr. Priestley observes, in favor of the story, "that all the parties seem to have been sufficiently void of fear, and also free from credulity, except the general belief that such things were supernatural." But he claims that where no good end is to be answered, we may safely conclude that no miracle was wrought.

To this Mr. Southey replies: "The former argument would be valid if the term miracle were applicable to the case; but by miracle Dr. Priestley evidently intends a manifestation of divine power, and in the present instance no such manifestation is supposed, any more than in the appearance of a departed spirit. Such things may be preternatural and yet not miraculous; they may be not in the ordinary course of nature, and yet imply no alteration of its laws. And with regard to the good end which they may be supposed to answer, it would be end sufficient if sometimes one of those unhappy persons, who, looking through the dim glass of infidelity, see nothing beyond this life, and the narrow sphere of mortal existence, should, from the well-established truth of one such story, (trifling and objectless as it might otherwise appear,) be led to a conclusion that there are more things in heaven and earth than are dreamt of in their philosophy."—*Southey's Life of Wesley*, pp. 24, 25.

Coleridge found a satisfactory solution of this knotty question in attributing the whole thing to a contagious nervous disease, with which he supposed the whole family to be afflicted, "the acme or intensest form of which is catalepsy." The poor dog, it seems, was as badly afflicted as the rest! This opinion does not need refutation.

Dr. Adam Clarke, who collected these accounts and published them in his *Wesley Family*, claims that the accounts given of these disturbances are so circumstantial and authentic as to entitle them to the most implicit credit. The eye and ear witnesses were persons of strong understandings and well-cultivated minds, untinctured by superstition, and in some instances rather skeptically inclined.

Dr. Clarke states that he and others of his particular acquaintances had been eye and ear witnesses of transactions of a similar kind, which could never be traced to any source of trick or imposture.

We have thus traced this spirit-commerce from the earliest times until the present. We have found little difficulty in identifying it in every period of its development. We have seen rappings, and trance-speaking, and doctors of medicine, and a great variety of physical phenomena, all in perfect accordance with what purports to be a new dispensation, just introduced under the name of Modern Spiritualism.

Dr. Hare asks, "Wherefore were not these efforts to communicate with mankind at an earlier period of the world's duration?" and then proceeds to argue that the world was not prepared for it. He says, "Two hundred years ago, Spiritualism would have been as much persecuted as witchcraft." But we have shown that the same efforts have been made to communicate with mankind, and that the witchcraft of "two hundred years ago is identical with the Spiritualism of to-day. There is no important point in which they differ."

We have found the developments of Spiritualism to be periodical. If the reader will mark well this fact, he may find less difficulty in determining its true character. There have been isolated cases in all ages, but the general outbreaks have been in connection with some great religious movement, coming immediately before and accompanying the same.

It seems to have made its appearance in an unusual manner just about the time the Son of God was revealed to destroy the works of the devil. After the ascension, we find it gradually waning until we lose sight of it almost entirely.

About the time of the Reformation, it burst upon Europe with unusual power; and wherever the Reformation spread, this unholy influence preceded and accompanied it, professing to be hostile to it.

Just before the "Great Awakening" in New England, we witness the terrible outbreak in Salem, and elsewhere in New England.

In England it makes a bold attack on the Wesley family, the prominent members of which were preparing to be leaders in the most wonderful and wide-spread religious movement of modern times.

The recent developments of Spiritualism preceded and accompanied one of the most remarkable revivals of religion ever known in Europe or America.

Spiritualism evidently belongs to that system of Satanic influences which have for the end the destruction of Christ's kingdom on earth. By its fruits it must be known, and to these we shall call the reader's attention in another chapter.

CHAPTER VII.

GOD'S TESTIMONY AGAINST SPIRITUALISM.

"There is, perhaps, no fact within the range of biblical science," says Rev. C. Munger, "in which critics are more agreed than in this, namely, that the word demon denotes a spiritual being, or that demons among the Greeks, Jews, and Christians, according to common belief and use, were spirits. . . . There is an entire unanimity among critics, so far as we have examined, in the fact named. . . . Whether the spirit is human or superhuman, is not so well agreed; neither is it at all material to our argument."

Without such an admission, so far as the Jews are concerned, the practice of Christ and his apostles can never be satisfactorily explained. If they did not regard the spirits, or demons, by them cast out, real existences, they intentionally misled the people.

We have shown that demons among the heathen were worshiped as the ghosts of departed heroes, conquerors, and potentates, and that popular superstition had deified them. Many of these demons were supposed to be evil spirits, while many of them were held in high esteem for their moral virtues. This was the heathen view. But the New Testament writers invariably use the term to denote evil spirits.

God has regarded the practice of consulting the dead with so much displeasure, that he has enacted stringent statutes against it. The thunderbolts of the divine displeasure are suspended over our heads at every step we take in this direction.

To seek unto mediums is to forsake God. We are to turn from them as from the path to hell.

The law declares, " There shall not be found among you a necromancer." Deut. xviii, 11. The people understood this to mean, " one who consulted disembodied spirits."

" A man also, or a woman, that hath a familiar

spirit, or that is a wizard, shall surely be put to death." Lev. xx, 27. Those who go after them to consult them are exposed to the divine displeasure: "And the soul that turneth after such as have familiar spirits, and after wizards, to go a whoring after them, I will even set my face against that soul, and will cut him off from among his people." Lev. xx, 6. Here the mediums, and those who consult them, are recognized as guilty of the same crime, and are exposed to the same punishment.

The sin of Babylon, and that which caused her ruin, was "the multitude of her sorceries, and the abundance of her enchantments." Isa. xlvii, 9. Her sorcerers, and astrologers, and stargazers, and monthly prognosticators, had no power to save her in the day of her visitation. "None shall save thee," (Isa. lxvii, 15,) was the final verdict.

One of the greatest sins of the wicked Manasseh, and that for which God cursed him and Israel, was, "He used enchantments, and dealt with familiar spirits and wizards," (2 Kings xxi, 6,) and thus seduced Israel to do more evil than the nations God had destroyed.

We have one mournful example in the scriptures for our warning, of a man turning from God to spirit-mediums. I refer to Saul.

The history says, "Saul died for his transgression which he committed against the Lord, even against the word of the Lord, which he kept not, and also for asking counsel of one that had a familiar spirit, to inquire of it; and inquired not of the Lord." 1 Chron. x, 13, 14.

Saul, like some who have gone out from us, when he was less corrupt, condemned spirit-commerce, and banished such as practiced it from his realm. (See 1 Sam. xxviii, 3.) But when he is fallen, and forsaken of God, he says, "Seek me a woman that hath a familiar spirit, that I may go to her, and inquire of her." 1 Sam. xxviii, 7. Disguised, and under cover of night, he goes to the medium and says, "Divine unto me by the familiar spirit, and bring me him up whom I shall name unto thee." 1 Sam. xxviii, 8. How forcibly is one reminded here of the Spiritualism of these times. The medium inquired, "Whom shall I bring up unto thee? And he said, Bring me up Samuel." 1 Sam. xxviii, 11. Now the spirits begin to hover around the spot. The medium said, "I saw gods," that is, demons or spirits, "ascending out of the earth." "Describe him," said Saul. "He is an old man, and is covered with a mantle." 1 Sam. xxviii, 12, 14.

The reason given by Saul for consulting Samuel, through the "woman that had a familiar spirit at En-dor," was, "I am sore distressed, for the Philistines make war against me, and God is departed from me, and answereth me no more, therefore I have called thee that thou mayest make known unto me what I shall do." 1 Sam. xxviii, 15. Samuel informed him that it was useless to consult him if God had forsaken him. If God was his enemy, he was not his friend.

Saul was guilty of rebellion against the government of God in taking the spoil of the Amalekites contrary to the express command of

10

God. This sin, called rebellion, the magnitude of which we can appreciate in these times, is said to be "as the sin of witchcraft." 1 Sam. xv, 23. For this sin "the Lord slew him."

To reason from analogy, we are forced to the conclusion, that modern Spiritualism is to the government of God, what southern rebellion is to the government of the United States. It is a direct blow at its heart to secure its destruction. It should be so regarded by every lover of truth and righteousness.

The New Testament, like the Old, is full of warning on this subject.

Paul declares that those who practice witchcraft, which all understood to be spirit-commerce, "shall not inherit the kingdom of God." Gal. v, 20, 21. Witchcraft is reckoned among the "works of the flesh," and opposed to the "fruit of the Spirit."

"Sorcerers shall have their part in the lake which burneth with fire and brimstone; which is the second death." Rev. xxi, 8.

"I would not that ye should have fellowship

with devils," says Paul. "Ye cannot drink the cup of the Lord and the cup of devils; ye cannot be partakers of the Lord's table and of the table of devils. Do ye provoke the Lord to jealousy? Are we stronger than he?" 1 Cor. x, 20, 21.

Rev. Mr. Munger has the following appropriate remarks on this passage: "We have before proved that the word here translated devils, is equivalent to our word 'spirits.' Also, that the spirits called up and consulted, and worshiped in the heathen feasts, were sometimes evil angels, but more commonly disembodied human spirits, such as are consulted in our modern circles at their 'tables.' The meaning of the apostle, then, seems to be this: 'I would not that ye should have fellowship with the spirits. Ye cannot be partakers of the Lord's table, and of the tables or circles where souls of the dead are evoked and consulted.'

"In short, he who accepts modern Spiritualism renounces Christianity, and God will renounce him. In the visions of John, we discover the sorcerers who made the lie and those who loved the lie, shut up in the same hell together."—*Ancient Sorcery*, etc., p. 66.

It is enough for us to know that these pretended revelations claim to contradict the oracles of God. Even Dr. Hare accuses those who disbelieve the mummeries of Spiritualism of "straining at the gnat of Spiritualism, yet swallowing the camels of Scripture."—P. 24. It is in this way that these professed religious reformers pour contempt upon that book which exposes and denounces their diabolical practices.

Directly against such bold and blasphemous pretensions, the apostle hurls the anathemas of Jehovah: "Though we, or an angel from heaven, preach any other Gospel unto you than that which we have preached unto you, let him be accursed." Gal. i, 8. So emphatic is the apostle on this subject that he repeats it in another form in the next verse, (verse 9:) "If any man preach any other Gospel unto you than that ye have received, let him be accursed." Still again, "If any man think himself to be a prophet, or spiritual, let him acknowledge that the things I write unto you are the commandments of the Lord." 1 Cor. xiv, 37.

We do not slander Spiritualism when we say it professes to preach a Gospel contrary to the word which Paul declares to be "the commandments of the Lord." There is no evading the conclusion; either the Bible is false, or the wrath of God is denounced against this whole system, with all its abettors and agents, and nothing but repentance and renunciation of their infernal commerce can save them from the execution of the fearful denunciation.

In the days of Jeremiah the spiritualists set themselves against God, and urged the people not to serve the king of Babylon. Jeremiah urged the people not to hearken unto their enchanters and sorcerers who say, "Ye shall not serve the king of Babylon, for they prophesy a lie unto you, to remove you far from your land." Jer. xxvii, 9, 10.

Isaiah warns the people against those who turn from the word of God, and seek counsel of the dead by means of spirit manifestations: "When they shall say unto you, Seek unto them that have familiar spirits, and unto wizards that peep and that mutter: should not a people seek unto their God? for the living to the dead? To the law and to the testimony: if they speak not according to this word, it is because there is no light in them." Isa. viii, 19, 20.

Dr. Clarke very properly renders the nineteenth verse, "Should not a nation seek unto its God? Why should you seek unto the dead concerning the living?"

Dr. Scott remarks, "But when the Jews were persuaded to seek unto such persons the prophet instructed them to inquire whether a people should not seek to their God, and whether it were right or reasonable to leave the living to consult the dead; the living God, to consult dead idols, or the spirits of dead men, whom these witches and wizards pretended to bring up to them. A strong expression of indignant abhorrence."—*In loco.*

How could Spiritualism be more clearly described? The operator, a witch, possessed of a familiar spirit, seeking through the agency of the spirits of dead men knowledge concerning the living or the dead; the seeker, a wicked dupe, induced to turn away from "the sure word of prophecy" to the uncertain and God-forbidden communications of demons.

Finally, observe among whom the practice of consulting the spirits of the dead prevailed. We find neither Abraham nor Moses, nor the true prophets, nor the apostles, nor any of the accepted people of God, seeking after spirits. But pagans, who never had revelation; the Canaanites, Egyptians, Chaldeans, Romans, and Greeks, apostates from God and his word; Saul, forsaken of God; Manasseh, the wicked king, and many others; these are the persons who were found seeking unto spirits.

In this particular the parallel holds good. To an almost incredible extent the spiritualists of the present day are composed of infidels, apostates from the Christian Church, and the most corrupt of mankind. (Rev. C. Munger.)

Spiritualism always appears as an enemy of God, and invariably in alliance with his enemies. Such was the fact in the days of Isaiah and Jeremiah, as well as in the days of Christ and the apostles. Such has been the fact with regard to each development of it to the present time. Its chief object seems to be to throw discredit upon the word of God, and scout the doctrines of the cross. It assaults heaven with the boldest blasphemies, stalks on with the most unblushing arrogance and presumption, and smokes and drips with corruption which would shock the morality of a heathen. These are the "gnats" of which Dr. Hare speaks, which are as nothing compared with the "camels of Scripture." So true it is that "wicked men and seducers wax worse and worse; deceiving and being deceived."

Mr. Howitt admits that the law of God was against consulting the spirits of the dead; but claims that Christ abrogated that law in seeking the spirit of Moses and Elias on the Mount of Transfiguration. Speaking of that event, he says, "It is the most remarkable case in the sacred history, because it demonstrates, and no doubt was planned by our Saviour to demonstrate that express abrogation of the Mosaic law regarding the spirits of the dead. Christ abrogated this law by himself seeking the spirit of Moses, the very promulgator of that law, and leading his disciples to do the same. . . . Christ went to seek this spirit, as if the case was studied literally. He might have commanded Moses to appear before him in his room; but no, as the law against seeking to the dead was to be abolished, he went to the spirit of the great dead, to Moses, the very man who prohibited such an act by the law in question, and there on the mount *broke* the law before his face, and by his example taught his disciples to do the same."—Vol. i, p. 218.

This is a very remarkable interpretation of a very plain account of the transfiguration. There is not the most distant intimation that Christ went up into the mountain to seek the spirits of Moses and Elias. The object for which he went upon the mountain is explicitly stated—to pray, and to be transfigured before them. While engaged in prayer, the fashion of his countenance was altered, so that his face shone as the sun, and his raiment was white as the light. In this state, it is said, Moses and Elias *appeared* unto him, and talked with him, not on the subject of the abrogation of the laws of Moses forbidding men to "seek unto spirits," but "of his decease which he should accomplish at Jerusalem." After the departure of Moses and Elias, there came a voice from the clouds, saying, not that the spirits are henceforth to instruct you, but, "This is my beloved Son: hear him!"

There are serious objections to Mr. Howitt's interpretation.

1. Nothing is said in the account about Christ's *seeking* the spirits of Moses and Elias. This was no more an abrogation of the law forbidding spirit commerce than the coming of angels to minister unto Christ after his temptation in the wilderness (Matt. iv, 11) was an abrogation of the law.

2. Nearly two years after the transfiguration, in the account given of the "rich man and Lazarus," Christ clearly vindicates the sufficiency of the holy Scriptures as a source of knowledge respecting the future world, and settles forever the question whether communications from the dead are of any practical utility in producing a pure life: "They have Moses and the prophets, let them hear them. And he said, Nay, but if one went to them from the dead, they will repent. And he said unto him, If they hear not Moses and the prophets, neither will they be persuaded, though one rose from the dead." How Christ could have abolished the law forbidding "seeking unto spirits," and then represent this spirit-commerce as utterly fruitless of good, we are unable to see.

3. This "seeking unto spirits," which Mr. Howitt admits is condemned by the law, but abrogated by Christ, is the same spirit-commerce which is condemned by the apostles. The Old Testament calls it *witchcraft*, and pronounces judgment against it. The apostle calls

it by the same name, and condemns it in the same manner. The Old Testament calls it *sorcery*, and writes condemnation against it. The apostle employs the same term, condemning it in like manner. They both mean by these terms one and the same thing—spirit-commerce. If the law against "seeking unto spirits" had been abolished by Christ, does any one suppose that the apostles would have pronounced the judgments of God upon those who continued in the practice?

4. Did it ever occur to the reader that the appearance of angels and spirits, sanctioned by the Scriptures, is in no way identical with the spirit manifestations of modern Spiritualism; while the "seeking unto spirits" by witches, etc., condemned by the Old and New Testaments, is in perfect keeping with modern Spiritualism? If God wishes to make important communications to Abraham he sends three angels, who appear unto him as he sits in the door of his tent as three men, and they talk with him. If God wishes to urge upon Lot the necessity of

his leaving Sodom he sends two angels, who appear to Lot as he sits in the gate of Sodom. If Moses and Elias are to be sent they come in human form, known even to the disciples. Many other cases might be mentioned. But the spirits evoked by spiritualists never appear in this manner. They come rapping or tipping, or using somebody's organs of speech besides their own.

The spirits whom God sends are never sought. Where in the Bible is a good man found "seeking unto spirits?" But witches and sorcerers invariably seek unto and call up spirits, who make their communications through these witches and sorcerers. Saul and the witch of En-dor is a case in point. This is the kind ot spirit-commerce answering to modern Spiritualism, which the Bible everywhere condemned. Mr. Howitt will not be able to make the candid reader believe that Christ has anywhere abro gated the law against spirit-commerce.

CHAPTER VIII.

FRUITS OF MODERN SPIRITUALISM.

EVERY religious system must be judged by its fruits. If it produce, legitimately, social disorder, and encourage personal corruption; if it seeks to remove all the barriers to vice, and openly sanctions contempt of divine authority, it is so far an unmixed evil that it should be discarded by every lover of God and humanity.

Mr. William Howitt (History of the Supernatural, p. 247) inquires how we are to distinguish "the true from the demoniac Spiritualism." His reply is, "By the divine rule; by the fruits they produce. That is the heavenly criterion which will guide every one who will attend to it as unerringly as the needle will guide the ship through the tempestuous and nocturnal seas, as the traveler through the pathless desert. So long as modern Spiritualism produces new and purer life, a firmer faith, a more fervent love of God and man, we may rest assured of its divine paternity; when it produces evil, it is as certainly from the devil."

We are prepared to accept or reject Spiritualism on this ground. We do not denounce Spiritualism as a corrupt system, because a few corrupt persons adhere to it; for in every religious order such persons are found. The system may be good, but these may be its *mis*representatives. But we are prepared to show that moral corruption is the legitimate fruit of Spiritualism, as a system. If it should produce good fruit, it would be "grapes of thorns and figs of thistles." Spiritualism has not one redeeming quality. We are yet to see the first person made better by it either in morals or religion; while the country is swarming with the victims of this spirit-commerce, ruined in reputation and morals, shunned as a moral pestilence by good men, and apparently forsaken of God, as those who have turned unto idols.

The views of the character of Christ and the

teachings of Revelation, entertained and promulgated by Spiritualists, cannot but be ruinous to the morals of any community embracing them. The most bitter and unscrupulous infidels of the past never spoke more disrespectfully of Christ and the Bible than do these new dispensation men, who live with one foot in this and the other in the spirit-world.

We propose to lay before our readers a brief view of the theology of Spiritualism, that they may judge of the correctness of the foregoing remarks.

We will introduce the testimony of Rev. T. L. Harris, for a long time a popular spiritualist, and hence a competent judge in the matters of which he speaks. Mr. Harris seeing the demoralizing tendency of the system abandoned it, and exposed its errors in a sermon preached in London, January 15th, 1860. He presents a clear, comprehensive, and truthful description of the doctrines held by spiritualists, and taught professedly by spirits from the unseen world. He says,

"First, that nature is God. Second, that God is an undeveloped principle in progress of evolution. Third, that the Jehovah of the Bible was an unprogressed, ferocious human spirit, who deceived ancient media. Fourth, that the Lord Christ was but a natural man, possessed of the ordinary mediumistic faculty of spiritual clairvoyance. Fifth, that our Lord's theological and psychical teachings were but the reproduction of false mythologies. Sixth, that he held his power, great or little, because under the influence of spirits of departed men.

"Shall we go further in this catalogue? We open, then, another series of spiritual teachings. "First, that all things originate in nature. Second, that man is a development of the animal. Third, that the first parents of the human race, born of brutes, were themselves but savages of the most degraded type. Fourth, that all things and beings are governed by natural necessity; that man possesses no freedom in the moral will. Fifth, that there is no retrogression, through moral disorders, either of the individual or of the species. Sixth, that vice is virtue in its unprogressed or germinal condition; that sin is an impossible chimera. Seventh, that self-love is the very center and fountain-head of all human affections, the chief inspirer of all human or spiritual actions. Eighth, that the spiritual world is but a theater for the continued evolution of human spirits, under the perpetual force of nature working through self-love.

"Or again, turn to another series: First, that the Scriptures are not the word of God, and that the divine Spirit never vouchsafed utterance to man. Second, that the Messiah, our Redeemer, is not in any sense a Saviour of the soul from sin, death, and hell. Third, that he never met in combat our spiritual foe; that he never overcame or cast out destroying spirits from their human slaves; that he never made an atonement or expiation for sin; that he never rose in his reassumed humanity from the grave; that he never ascended, glorified, to heaven; that he never communicated the Holy Ghost.

"Or again, to another: That there is no judgment to come beyond the grave, wherein the Lord shall adjudge the departed according to their deeds, the good to eternal life, the evil to everlasting punishment and the second death. That all men, irrespective of formed character for evil here, become the delighted and immortal inhabitants of a perpetual elysium. That broad is the way and wide is the gate that leadeth unto life eternal, and that none can help to find it.

"Or again: and now as touching a moral point of social interest. Spirits declare that there is no marriage as a natural law, but that polygamy or bigamy are as orderly as the monogamic tie. But if this be not frequently inculcated, what shall we say to the broadly put forth declaration of spirits, that the marital tie is the result of natural affinity, and that where two are legally conjoined, and the wandering inclinations of either rove to another object, the new attraction becomes the lawful husband or wife?"—*Harris's Sermon*, pp. 5–7.

Mr. Harris concludes in the following language:

"I pledge myself, and stand committed to the assertion, that through mediumistic channels, all these things are taught as emanating from the spirits; and worse is taught, if possible, to those who penetrate the inner circles of the gloomy mysteries, where the old magic is born again."

An association of individuals holding and advocating such views cannot but be a curse to any community in which they may exist. Such principles are absolutely demoralizing.

We will permit spiritualists to speak for themselves, then we shall not be accused of misrepresenting their views.

SPIRITUALISTIC VIEW OF SIN.

Dr. Hare, an oracle among the Spiritualists, says, "The prodigious diversity between virtue and vice is the consequence of contingencies, which are no more under the control of the individual affected, than the color of his hair or the number of cubits in his stature."

Again, "There is no evil that can be avoided." The meaning of all this is, a man may steal your purse, rob your house, murder your wife, or ruin your daughter; he may be found a drunkard in a rum-shop, a bacchanalian in a brothel, a convict in a prison, or a bloody criminal on a gallows, and his crimes are no more his own acts than the color of his hair, or the height of his growth.

These views of Dr. Hare are in perfect keeping with revelations made professedly by spirits. He says, "Such an inference coincides with the communications recently received from the spirits of departed friends." In view of such necessity to wrong action, Dr. Hare claims that Christ has imposed upon us "excessive and impracticable restraints."

I do not wonder that such a moral teacher should declare, "The Bible of the spiritualists is the book of nature, the only one which by inward and outward evidence can be ascribed to divine authorship."

Miss Lizzie Doten, a popular spiritualist, says, "Whatever man does, he but works out through the mediumship of Deity."—*Banner of Light*, February 8, 1862.

In view of such a faith the following prayer is appropriate, (Banner of Light, December 3, 1862,) "We thank thee for all conditions of men, for the drunkard, for the prostitute, for the dissolute of every description."

Spiritualists claim that wickedness and morality alike help on their cause, and hence they have no word of condemnation for the former, or approval for the latter. A writer in the "Banner of Light," January 18, 1862, says,

"I have no reply for those who tell me such a one does wickedly, or such a one holds erroneous sentiments; that one is in free love, another in atheism; for there is not an act done, not a sentiment entertained, not a freak of free love, nor a frozen blast of atheism . . . that does not help on the grand and glorious superstructure."

A writer in the same paper, February 8, 1862, says,

"In all, too, that I have written upon the all-right subject, I hope there is not to be found anything that deals condemnation and blame to any of the deeds done by humanity. Humanity acts by the force of its own inherent, invisible power, the same as the earth revolves by its own inherent, invisible power of revolution-or as the vegetable world sends forth its tints of beauty in a thousand kinds and forms, all from the inherent nature of the germs that make these kinds and forms."

The writer continues: "I cannot think that libertinism injures the immortal soul of man."

One would suppose that these were the sentiments of abandoned libertines, who were seeking under cover of religion to practice deeds of darkness. But spirits professedly teach the same. "We declare," says a spirit, (Banner of Light, March 8, 1862,) "there never was an individual spirit that trespassed upon the smallest portion of God's law."

In the "Banner of Light," October 29, 1859, we have the report of a discussion by a Convention of Spiritualists:

"*Question.* Are the manifestations of human life that we call evil, or sinful, a necessity of the conditions of the soul's progress?

"*Dr. Child.* From the deepest and most sincere convictions of my soul, I answer to the question: That what we call sin and evil in human actions *is a necessity*, and, being a necessity, it is lawful and right. This view of the question is in harmony with all evil; it sees all that is wrong and repulsive to the soul's higher longings, as being the effects of a means in the ordering of Divine Wisdom, for the production of the greatest possible good for humanity. It sees darkness as necessary as light in the spiritual as well as in the physical world. . . . It recognizes the hand of God in the serpent's venom as much as in the fragrance of the pure water-lily; in the crude granite, as full and perfect as in the existence of angel-life. It sees all the manifestations of life, both good and bad, as being the immediate effect of nature's laws, which laws are the laws of God—laws that were never broken, and never can be; laws, every jot and tittle of which, as Christ has said, must be fulfilled. . . . It sees the manifestation of every human soul, whether good or bad, as being the necessary result of a certain condition, in which condition is to be found a natural cause that produced the good or bad action. Judas, the traitor, was as faithful to the condition of his being as was St. John, the divine—each performed the mission assigned to each, lawfully and truly. Behind the holy deeds of Fenelon there existed natural causes that produced them; he could not help the manifestations of good. Behind the dark deeds of King Herod, the enemy of Christ, there existed natural causes that produced the wicked deeds of his life; he could not help them. In Fenelon there is no merit; in Herod there is no demerit. There are no laudations for Fenelon, and no condemnation for Herod. There is no comparison to be made between the two; no judgment to be instituted. Fenelon is a child of God: Herod is the same—each heirs of eternal life and the blessings of God that await them in the coming future. Fenelon is no nearer to God than Herod is. . . . The affirmative accepts every opinion and every creed, and not only opinions and creeds, but every deed of goodness and every deed of evil, as being necessary and right, that ever existed in the great family of humanity.

"*Mr. Newton* said: I shall not deny that evils and sins of the descriptions mentioned are for the most part *necessary*, in the constitution of things, to growth or progress. Plainly there can be no PROGRESS unless there is a *lower* as well as a *higher*. There is no attaining to perfection, unless there is an imperfection to begin with. All such *evils* are merely *lesser goods*. Nor, again, do I deny, that the road through hell—even the 'lowest hell'—may lead eventually to heaven; nor that those who travel that way and reach the celestial city at last, through crimes and miseries and agonies untold, will not have a larger capacity for happiness and for usefulness in saving others than the merely innocent, the passively good, whose robes were never stained even by *contact* with the vile. None of these positions shall I deny, *for I honestly believe them true.*

"*H. F. Gardner.* Dr. Child has got more philosophy in his ideas of good and evil than most people ever thought of. The world ought to know and feel the necessity, the blessing of sin. Jesus and Judas both had the experience they needed, and neither were made better or worse by the simple acts they were compelled to do by their innate condition.

"*Mr. Wilson,* of New York: I am with my friend, Dr. Child, for his views come nearest to the standard of true Christianity of any I ever heard; they are but a reiteration of the philosophy taught eighteen hundred years ago. Moral distinctions I cannot recognize as an essential quality of the soul.

"*Miss Lizzie Doten,* (*entranced.*) Evil is evil only by comparison. . . . Why does he (pointing to Dr. Child) present such views? It is because the philanthropy of his large heart wants to take all humanity to heaven, the wicked and the suffering, as well as the good and the happy. He would take even the devil himself to heaven, and it may be that the devil will have a seat in heaven; that God will say, 'Take, Lucifer, thy place. This day art thou redeemed to archangelic state.'

"The views of Dr. Child are broad and comprehensive; he goes for generals. His views are right, his position is true. In this general view the wisdom of Providence is seen in its perfection; there is *no evil*, *no sin;* but when you come to minutiæ, with limited perception, you see evil. God produced everything good at first, and God has never changed his mind; everything is good still."

Here we find Fenelon and Herod, Judas and Christ, equal unto the angels; sin a blessing, moral distinctions annihilated, and Lucifer on his way to heaven.

These are samples of the spiritualistic view of sin. Views, it seems to us, more in conflict with common sense, more revolting to morality, more at war with the potent barriers to vice, and more directly calculated to overturn all well-regulated society, never fell from the lips of infidel or demon. If these be the doctrines of spirits, as claimed by spiritualists, they must be what Saint Paul calls "doctrines of devils," from which all should turn away.

SPIRITUALISTIC VIEW OF CHRIST.

The manner in which spiritualists speak of the Saviour amounts to little less than blasphemy.

The "Banner of Light, December 8, 1861, says, "Once mankind clung to the cross, and adored the form of Him who was crucified on Calvary, as a God. But reason has asserted its supremacy, and the world has declared it would not have this man to reign over it any longer."

One is strikingly reminded of the language of the Saviour in speaking of himself: Luke xix. "A certain nobleman went into a far country, to receive for himself a kingdom, and to return. And he called his ten servants, and delivered them ten pounds, and said unto them, Occupy till I come. But his citizens hated him, saying, We will not have this man to reign over us." When he returned, of these last he said, "But those mine enemies, which would not that I should reign over them, bring hither, and slay them before me."

Julian the Apostate reproached Christ while living, but when dying he exclaimed, "O Galilean, thou hast conquered."

The same mouth-piece of Spiritualism continues: "Thus Jesus has become only a man, stripped of all false pretensions, and we have even aspired to stand by his side on the Mount of Calvary." The Jews once stood by his side on the Mount of Calvary, but it was only to give utterance to the malice of the human heart in "Crucify him, crucify him!"

Emma Harding, a popular medium of Spiritualism, inquires, "What evidence have we that Christ is the Lord of Spirits? has any sort of influence upon our hereafter, or even has an objective existence at all? . . . Science, sense, and reason prove to me, that my dead father lives. . . . Why should I doubt him when he tells me he sees no Jesus in his hereafter, knows none? . . . When the testimony of thousands of spirits is confirmatory of my father's experience, and I never yet met with one of the redeemed by the merits of Jesus, and never yet saw a fact in Spiritualism which proved any such redemption, nor met with any medium who could prove any such spirit, I still maintain my position."—*Banner of Light*, December 28, 1861.

A spirit, calling herself Martha Hutchins, makes the following statement, (Banner of Light, March 1, 1852:) "My father was a Christian, but I was not. There are no Christians here; they don't believe in anything like they used to when they came here."

It may be easily shown why the spirits who communicate with spiritualistic mediums have never seen Christ, or known him as a Redeemer, in the world from which they come, as neither he nor the redeemed reside in that world. "Without are sorcerers and idolaters, and whosoever loveth and maketh a lie." "Where I am," says Jesus, "there shall my servants be." But to the wicked, "Whither I go, ye cannot come." This is the evidence that these communications, if from spirits, are from demons damned. They find neither Jesus the Redeemer, nor Christians the redeemed, in the world to which their sins have consigned them.

Stephen and John had a very different view of Jesus and the redeemed. While dying, Stephen looked upward and saw heaven opened, and Jesus sitting at the right hand of God, and he prayed, "Lord Jesus receive my spirit," and passed away.

John had a view of Jesus and the souls he had redeemed in the heaven which opened upon his vision. Their songs were full of Jesus and redemption: "Worthy is the Lamb to receive riches, and honor, and power; for thou wast slain, and hast redeemed us to God by thy blood, out of every kindred, people, and nation."

Stephen and John claim to have seen heaven. They claim to have seen Jesus in that world.

Spiritualists say, "There is not a fact in Spiritualism going to show the existence of any such person" in the world from which their communications come.

St. John claims to have seen a great multitude who had been redeemed by the blood of Jesus. Spiritualists say they never met with a *redeemed* spirit, and there is not a fact in Spiritualism going to prove the existence of any such spirit. The simple inference from all this is, that Stephen and John had a view of one world and spiritualists of another; one of heaven, the other of hell; one of spirits redeemed, the other of spirits damned; showing most conclusively that spiritualists have departed "from the faith, giving heed to seducing spirits and doctrines of devils."

SPIRITUALISTIC VIEW OF HELL.

Spiritualists descant upon the doctrine of future punishment and the existence of hell with feelings amounting to holy horror. A distinguished spiritualist says, "I need not remind the thinker what sort of a *father* grows out of the idea of hell." And yet, strange to say, they propose to go through hell to reach heaven: making it a half-way house in their journey.

Miss Doten says, "Heaven, hell, and earth are but three indissoluble degrees contiguous to each other. We must go through hell to reach heaven. We cannot leave earth without going to hell first, for that is the ante-chamber to heaven."—*Banner of Light*, Dec., 1861.

The rich man of the Scriptures left earth in the same direction which spiritualists propose to take. He met in his way an impassable gulf. Seeing his folly, he proposed to send back a messenger, and warn his friends not to come that way. But he was informed that if his friends would not heed the warnings of the sacred Word they would not be persuaded to change their course by what a spirit from the dead might say to them. As spiritualists propose to take the same road which their ancient friend took, even now that the spirits *have* returned, the evidence is conclusive that Abraham was correct in his judgment of the matter.

In view of such sentiments, it is not difficult to explain the friendly relations which exist, professedly, between spiritualists and the devil. It is prudent to secure the friendship of those through whose country we propose to journey.

It may appear strange, but it is nevertheless true, that spiritualists offer prayer to the devil. As an evidence of this, read the following from the "Banner of Light," March 1, 1862:

"INVOCATION.

"O thou prince of darkness and king of light, god and devil, greater and lesser good, perfect and imperfect being! we ask and demand of thee that we may know thee, for to know thee is to know more of ourselves. And if to do this it be necessary to wander in hell, yea and amen, we will wander there with the spirits of darkness. The Church and the world tell us that the devil goeth about like a roaring lion, seeking whom he may devour, but we know thee only as God's vicegerent, to stand at his left hand, the regenerator of mankind, the means of bringing up all things, intellectually and morally, to perfection."

Lizzie Doten offered the following prayer at Lyceum Hall, Boston, Dec. 8, 1861. Reported for the "Banner of Light," and published in that paper, Dec. 21, 1861:

INVOCATION.

"O Lucifer, thou sun of the morning, who fell from thy high estate, and whom mortals are prone to call the embodiment of evil, we lift our voices unto thee. We know that thou canst not harm us unless by the will of the Almighty, of whom thou art a part and portion, and in whose economy thou playest thy part; and we cannot presume to sit in judgment over Deity. From the depths of thine infamy streams forth divine truth. Why should we turn from thee? Does not the same inspiration rule us all? Is one in God's sight better than another? We know thou art yet to come up in his expanded creation, purified by the influence of God's love, for his love is not perfected while one of his children writhes in misery. So, O Lucifer, do we come up and stand before the throne of the Ancient of Days, hand in hand with thee. As thou hast been the star of the morning, thou wilt again become an angel of light. O, Satan, we will subdue thee with our love, and thou wilt yet kneel humbly with us at the throne of God."

A person unacquainted with the theory and practice of spiritualists might regard this as a burlesque upon Spiritualism; but we must remember that this is a sober address to Satan, in the presence of a Boston audience, in the year 1861, by one of the most popular mediums in New England.

Spiritualism can lay claim to nothing new, however, in its special friendship for and worship of the devil. Pagans have the start of them. Devil-worship has been systematized in

Ceylon, Burmah, and many parts of the East Indies; and an order of devil-priests has existed even in modern times. Mr. Ives, in his travels through Persia, gives an account of the devil-worship among the Sanjacks, a nation inhabiting the country about Mosul, the ancient Nineveh. This strange people once professed Christianity, then Mohammedanism, and finally Devilism. There is a remarkable identity, in faith and practice, between these strange people and spiritualists. Mr. Ives says, "They say it is true that the devil has at present a quarrel with God; but the time will come when, the pride of his heart being subdued, he will make his submission to the Almighty; and as the Deity cannot be implacable, the devil will receive a full pardon for all his transgressions, and both he and all those who paid him attention during his disgrace will be admitted into the blessed mansions. This is the foundation of their hope, and this chance for heaven they esteem to be a better one than that of trusting in their own merits, or the merits of the leader of any religion whatsoever. The person of the devil they look on as sacred. Whenever they speak of him, it is with the utmost respect."

Who can question for a moment but that Spiritualism is from beneath, and that all who adhere to it are guilty of devil-worship? Are not these the unclean spirits which came out of the mouth of the dragon and false prophets? (Rev. xvi, 13, 14.) They were "the spirits of devils working miracles."

SPIRITUALISTIC VIEW OF THE MARRIAGE RELATION.

Spiritualists seek professedly to pull down and destroy all existing institutions. It seeks to lay its fiendish hand upon all the safeguards of social life, and remove every barrier to the gratification of their prejudices or passions. Governments are to become a Babel of ruins; Church and State are to become true yoke-fellows; religious organizations are to crumble at its touch; and a beautiful structure, "full of corruption and dead men's bones," is to take their place.

With regard to the marriage relation, so far as they think it prudent to divulge their real views, they are outspoken. Their view of this relation may be inferred from a sentiment put forth at a wedding in Charlestown, Mass., Nov. 20, 1861: "Legal marriage, practically, is selfish, carnal, worldly-minded, and belongs to mammon."

Referring to the marital relation, under the head of "social questions," a writer in the "Banner of Light" says, "If spiritualists ever accomplish the work assigned them, they must no longer ask to wink out of sight those great social questions underlying the foundations of true life. If our social or affectional relations are wrong we must seek to right them, and render them pure, true, and harmonic, or all our efforts in other directions will prove abortive. It is worse than nonsense for us to falter for the sake of reputation, popularity, or false public opinion. [Reputation, it seems, is of no account with spiritualists.] These are shams. . . . Millions of hearts are now breaking, bursting, or rising in rebellion. All false unions are being fearfully shaken and sundered. No wonder at the alarm of timid, selfish, conservative, sordid souls. Many dangers are threatened, but these are inevitable to all great revolutions. . . . But hells must have an airing, and the sunlight of the spheres be let in. Many sad, unfortunate, social disruptions may ensue, but all these things are essential, as experiences to impart lessons of wisdom and prudence.

"Spiritualism will become the living gospel of the age only so far as its believers begin to practice its principles, regardless of policy or reputation, . . . let the cost, the sacrifice, be what it may. Come, brothers and sisters, who dare begin?"

I understand this writer to mean that all marital relations which are not perfectly harmonious should at once be dissolved. No matter how much ruin may result to wife and children, and whole households; no matter how much sadness and misfortune may result from such social disruptions; these are essential to the accomplishment of the end sought by Spiritualism. Instead of hell's having an airing by the advancement of such views, hell holds jubilee at the removal of all the safeguards to domestic happiness.

John M. Spear, at a lecture in Utica, N. Y., delivered himself of the following anathema:

"Cursed be the marriage institution; cursed be the relation of husband and wife; cursed be all who would sustain legal marriage! What if there are a few tears shed, or a few hearts broken? They only go to build up a great principle, and all great truths have their martyrs."

A correspondent of the "Spiritual Telegraph," in referring to an unmarried woman who had recently become a mother, commends her for the course, regarding it as a signal triumph of a spiritualistic principle. He says:

"It is reserved for this our day, under the inspiration of the spirit-world, for a quiet, equable, retiring woman to rise up in the dignity of her womanhood, and declare in the face of her oppressors and a scowling world, I will be free! God helping me, though I stand alone, penniless, friendless, homeless, forsaken of all. I will exercise that dearest of all rights, the holiest and most sacred of all heaven's gifts—the right of maternity—in the way which to me seemeth right; and no man, nor set of men; no Church, no State, shall withhold from me the realization of that purest of all aspirations inherent in every true woman, the right to re-beget myself when, and by whom, and under such circumstances, as to me seem fit and best."

We might multiply quotations from spiritualists on this subject, but there can be no doubt but Spiritualism seeks to remove all the old landmarks which have been set up for the defense of morality, religion, and good order among men. It seeks to let loose a horde of lecherous, religious mountebanks upon the community, such as "creep into houses and lead captive silly women, laden with sins, led away with divers lusts;" "men of corrupt minds, reprobate concerning the truth." 2 Tim. iii, 6, 8.

Already hundreds of homes, once happy, have been turned into earthly hells, filled with untold horrors; fathers and husbands wandering in the mazes of Spiritualism in search of some Jezebel who "calleth herself a prophetess," while wife and children are left to poverty, shame, and disgrace. Spiritualism glories in this work, claims to be called of God to it, and is resorting to every means that can be invented by the most subtle ingenuity of depraved minds to accomplish its object.

Their practice is fully up to their theory. A writer having been for some time identified with Spiritualism, but renouncing it, made the following statement some three years ago: "We have more than four hundred public mediums and spiritual lecturers in the northern states. At least three hundred of them have been married. Nearly one half of these have absolved their conjugal relations; a large proportion of the remainder are living in the most discordant relations, having abandoned the bed of their partners, and by mutual consent of many, living in promiscuous concubinage."

We could register the names of many who, before they became spiritualists, were happy in the enjoyment of domestic life; but now their families are broken up, and desolation reigns where happiness once smiled. I charge spiritualists with being guilty of the outrage. It is what they advocate, and what their doctrine of spiritual affinities implies. It is an outrage on society, and every man who sustains it says, in so doing, that whenever his inclinations or lusts lead him from the wife he has sworn to love, to unite himself to a paramour, he is authorized by his creed, yea, by the teaching of the spirits, to do so.

It may be objected by some that we have only spoken of evil spirits. This is true. But we have spoken of all the spirits which Spiritualism has evoked, good and bad. "A good tree cannot bring forth evil fruit. Wherefore, by their fruit ye shall know them." A system which produces such fruits as we have described and shall further describe is an unmixed evil, and cannot have the support of God or good angels. The devil can change himself into an angel of light, and by "signs, and lying wonders, and deceivableness of unrighteousness," quite stagger the faith of the elect.

We have witnessed its phenomena, seen tables tip, seen writing executed in a mysterious manner, heard trance speakers, etc., and from the first observations made, we have been convinced of its Satanic character.

CHAPTER IX.

TESTIMONY AGAINST SPIRITUALISM.

THE following testimonies against Spiritualism are from persons who have been identified with the system, and among its prominent supporters. They have witnessed its workings behind the curtain, and seen its influence upon its mediums and chief advocates. They have been driven, by witnessing its terrible fruits, to abandon the system, and to warn others of the danger of spirit-commerce.

The first is from Mr. William Fishbough, several years editor of the "Spiritual Telegraph," scribe of Andrew Jackson Davis's "Nature's Divine Revelation," and popularly known as a prominent spiritualist of the highest order. The authors of "Mysterious Noises" say he is "one of the most philosophical observers of the various phenomena of the human mind, and a well-known psychological writer," and "editor of the Univercœlum," etc. His testimony as to the influence of Spiritualism may be found in the following paragraph, written June 25th, 1860:

"While I firmly believe that God has overruled it from the first for the accomplishment of wise and beneficent purposes, and that its phenomena, when religiously studied in the light of the divine word, will settle some very important points of psychological and pneumatic science, I am compelled to say that its great leading doctrines and philosophizing, when viewed in the abstract, are an attack, either open or covert, upon all that is vital in religion, and upon all the more potent barriers to vice and social disorder that are provided by the law; and that if its tendencies could remain unchecked, the result would be a dissolution of all the chief bonds of society. I am, moreover, constrained to warn all men, on peril of the most fatal consequences, against seeking the aid of 'Beelzebub, the god of Ekron,' or of any other demon, so long as there is a 'God in Israel.' 2 Kings i, 2–6."

THE TESTIMONY OF WM. B. COAN.

Mr. Coan is, or was, the husband of A. L. Coan, the celebrated rapping and test medium. Mrs. Coan is said to have left her husband, and to have taken up a life of promiscuous prostitution, for which he obtained a divorce. He formerly traveled from Maine to Minnesota, in company with his wife, giving "tests of spiritual identity," and was engaged in the business for about six years. He says, in a letter to a friend:

"DEAR SIR,—In reply to your request for my opinion of modern Spiritualism, I will say, I consider it a great and dangerous delusion; the greatest curse that ever visited this or any other people; a destroyer of religion, domestic peace, and the moral sense of its victims, and leading finally to licentiousness and prostitution. It has already broken up more families in this country than all other causes combined. It leads its victims on step by step until they commit enormities, under the belief that they are doing God's service, the very thought of which would have been revolting to them before they were caught in its intoxicating snare.

"Fraternally yours, WM. B. COAN.

"NEW YORK, *June* 27, 1861."

THE TESTIMONY OF B. F. HATCH, M.D.

Dr. Hatch is the husband of Cora L. V. Hatch, the popular trance-medium. He was for a long time a prominent spiritualist, and is well qualified to testify with regard to its doctrines and moral influence. He has been shamefully abused by spiritualists since he has attempted to expose their wickedness; but the facts stated are known and read of all men who have any knowledge of Spiritualism.

Having had several private conversations with Dr. Hatch on the subject of Spiritualism, I requested him to give me, in writing, a brief statement of his views on the subject. The following letter was received in reply. It must be confessed that the picture is a dark one, but it is no darker than the facts will justify.

"Rev. W. M'Donald:

"Dear Sir,—You ask for a brief statement of my observation and experience of modern Spiritualism, which for the benefit of the public I am most happy to give. In its early history, having for several years been a public advocate of the doctrine of universal salvation, I was prepared to accept the claims of Spiritualism as being angelic, and it is well known that for several years I did much to establish it on this basis. For a while its real character and nature were hid amid extravagant pretensions of the blessings to result from 'these heavenly messengers visiting earth's inhabitants;' and in its early development we saw but little, comparatively, of the mischievous effects that are now everywhere so conspicuous.

"Suffice it to say that the horde of damned spirits which still linger amid the scenes of their former wickedness, Proteus-like, assuming any and every form to accomplish their hellish purpose, soon demonstrated, not only the falsity of my previous faith, but also the terrible danger of carrying on a forbidden commerce with the unseen world. As it commanded attention through the powerful demonstrations of the physical phenomena, and public confidence by false pretensions, it became more and more unmasked as to its real tendency, until now the drama of the basest iniquity is freely and, in many instances, openly enacted before the bewildered gaze of the public. To-day its mischievous and corrupting effects are limited only by the capability of human depravity. There is now a class of necromancers or earthly devils, denominated mediums, (and they are the most favorably known in the spiritualistic ranks,) whose secret crimes excel in real wickedness those of Messalina and the Borgias. This statement, extravagant as it may appear, I stand pledged as a man of honor to fully demonstrate whenever called upon to do so.

"I will rehearse some of the leading doctrines of Spiritualism, as I gather them in private conversation, and from their oral speeches and publications. In holy reverence commit your soul to God while you read.

"God is irreverently called the 'old man who seduced Mary and begat Christ the bastard.' Christ, a very well-meaning but ignorant Jewish gentleman, who manifested his goodness of heart in forgiving the adulteress woman, but exposed his ignorance of human needs when he requested her to sin no more. The apostles were very good mediums, but too much biased by the ignorance and superstitions of their cotemporaries. The Bible, which means 'excellent soft bark,' will do for an imbecile and unenlightened people, but is superseded by the spiritual philosophy. Self-love is the throne of God within, and should be obeyed.

"Marriage is universal, and knows no limit but desire, has no moral binding force, and should be adhered to only by such as are willing to be slaves, as the law of affinity transcends all institutions. The right to choose a different father for each and every successive offspring 'is inherent in every true woman,' and the intimate relation of husband and wife should precede marriage as a preliminary means of judging of their fitness to each other. All lustful desires should be ultimated, as this becomes the means of their purification. Cursings are but the dross of human nature, and are blessings to him who uses them. Blaspheming God is a purifying process of the soul. 'Every curse (Banner of Light, April 28, 1860) escaping the lips of the profane one is a blessing to him; it is casting off evil in the spirit-sparks from the fire, which will purify the spirit.'

"Murder but hurries the victim to heaven and blesses the murderer. Vice in every form is equally meritorious with virtue, as there is no moral responsibility. Sin is an impossible chimera. Chastity is a name with no other meaning than bondage to barbarous institutions. And life with all its varied scenes is but a prelude of that drama to be played beyond the valley of the shadow of death.

"Need I say that their practices are fully in keeping with this creed? This is painfully demonstrated wherever they have gained any foothold. Some of the most prominent spiritualists have confessed that the strongest bond of union among them is the facility their association affords for sexual debauchery.

"Every woman, so far as I know, (and I know of many,) who yields herself to spirit-influence leads a meretricious life; and I seriously question there being any exception to this rule, for the latter is the legitimate result of the former.

"In our municipal courts we have no protection against this pernicious people.

"On more occasions than one I have known one after another, under the sanctity of an oath, deliberately fabricate the basest falsehood without any perceptible compunctions of conscience. I most solemnly affirm that during several years' acquaintance with the leading spiritualists of this country, I have never been able to discover among them any other standard of morality than a fidelity to their wickedness. Notwithstanding that most of their public advocates are men and women stripped of every virtue, and many of them openly living in adulterous relations, and murdering the embryo offsprings of their own guilt, not one of them, to my knowledge, has ever received a rebuke from their journals or confederates in principles.

"But those who have left them, and rebuked their abominations, because they could not brook them, have been made to feel their invectives and slander as if vomited forth from all pandemonium. In no single instance have I known of any improvement (neither do I expect it) in the moral or religious life of its votaries, but uniformly its tendency has been to bewilder the judgment and corrupt the life, until all moral distinctions are ignored. And what is still worse to relate, they conjoin their wickedness with their religion, and by this means destroy the action of conscience, and thus become wholly deprived of all perceptions of right, given over to hardness of heart, and abandoned of God. In this state, with the power of reason destroyed, the passions lashed into wild and untamable fury, without restraint, they sow to the wind, while hurrying on to their places among the damned, to reap the whirlwind.

"Fraternally yours, B. F. HATCH.

"PROVIDENCE, R. I., *November*, 1861."

THE TESTIMONY OF MR. J. F. WHITING.

Mr. Whiting was for some time a very prominent spiritualist in the city of New York, and was one of the getters up and chief supporters of what are known as the "Broadway Rooms," for the propagation of Spiritualism. After witnessing its immoral tendencies for some time he abandoned it.

The letter is addressed to Dr. Hatch, and, to some extent, confirms his statements.

"DEAR SIR,—Your letter, dated Providence, R. I., May 28th, 1860, is before me, requesting me to give you some facts relative to the evil effects of modern Spiritualism. My time is so much occupied with business matters that I have very little opportunity to interest myself upon the subject, or to draw legitimate conclusions as to its terrible and damning results upon its believers, especially its mediums. It is hardly necessary for me to give you any facts relating to such a topic. Your lengthened and extensive experience among the better classes and more enlightened circles of spiritualists has given you great opportunities to see the rascality and sin which the majority of its believers have been addicted to. We have the fact daily spread before us in the public journals throughout the country of the fruits of Spiritualism; and there is hardly a town or village in the land but can produce plenty of facts demonstrating the damning tendency and ruinous consequences which arise from this forbidden intercourse with spirits.

"I look upon modern Spiritualism as the work of Satan, and which has created more sin and iniquity since its introduction through the Fox family than all other crimes and vices during the last fifty years. In short, from what experience I have with Spiritualism and its believers, I am firmly convinced that the result of Spiritualism is, as I have said before, wholly immoral and debasing; destroying all the moral character of its believers, inculcating as it does false principles, and raising false hopes, thereby rendering man little better than the brute creation. Adultery, fornication, deception, and hypocrisy are its leading tendencies. The spirits assume the garb of angels, while in fact they are but devils doomed by sin on earth, and seek through Spiritualism to increase their power in hell by converts from the earth.

"I have known many spiritual mediums, and I am free to confess that I hardly ever found one who on a thorough examination could stand the test of truth, virtue, or honesty. They fail either in one or the other of these traits of character. I am deeply impressed with the fact that modern Spiritualism is the work of spirits; but they are evil ones, and I can see no good resulting from holding communion with them.

"Yours very truly, J. F. WHITING."

We conclude these testimonials against Spiritualism with one from the very heart of the spiritualistic ranks. This, I trust, will be acceptable to spiritualists, although dealing a heavier blow against it for its practical corruptions than any we have introduced.

THE TESTIMONY OF MRS. CORA L. V. HATCH.

Mrs. Hatch is one of the most popular mediums to be found among spiritualists. Seeing the corrupting influence of the system upon the polluted infidel hordes who embrace it, she makes a bold attempt at reforming them. A hopeless task!

In a lecture delivered in New York city, January 19, 1862, entitled "Spiritualism, its Theory and Practice," she says:

"There is no doubt that the shaft which Spiritualism has sunk has struck the vein ot that floating population in the United States and other countries, of which we have spoken in terms which are no less applicable to their mental and spiritual than to their political status. They form a class who have never believed in anything, but are ready to adopt any form of belief, as occasion may require, from orthodox Christianity down to the latest ism. They are the aids and reliance of the radical reformers, the destructives, who tear down old edifices indiscriminately, and put up nothing in their stead. They considered themselves commissioned to reform the world. They decry Christianity, and all other supports of law and order recognized by society. They have been ready to seize upon any new doctrine, and it is not at all surprising that Spiritualism, which presents such an admirable cover for their designs, should have attracted many of these characters, and that in their hands it has become one of the most preposterous systems, both as to theory and practice, ever brought before the community. . .

"Thus it happens that we have as advocates of Spiritualism all the offscourings of society in a new shape. We have the *ci-devant* apostles of Mormonism, Fourierism, and every other 'reform' movement which nobody has cared to adopt; and when the world recognizes these as leaders in our ranks it stands aghast and says, 'Why, these are the old nuisances revived. This Spiritualism is but another name for that which leads to immorality, and the tearing down of all that is dear and sacred in our institutions. It opposes Christianity, and even seeks to violate the sanctity of the fireside;' and we are sorry to state that the conduct of those in general who profess to be spiritualists confirms this judgment, and society has too good ground for complaint and apprehension. It must be so from what we have stated. . . . The general tendencies of Spiritualism have been not to elevate but degrade its disciples in the moral and social scale, to break down all barriers which have been considered essential to a well-ordered community, and destroy every altar and shrine to which their rites and sacrifices could not be admitted. Each member of the class to which we refer seizes hold of Spiritualism with the same idea—that he or she is to be made the savior of humanity by its means. Every broken-down politician or expelled church-member seeks to engraft upon it his own audacious speculations, and to make spirits responsible for what he dare not openly advocate in his own person. . . . If you have any doubt of this you have but to look abroad over the land."

Spiritualists have stoutly denied that the fruits of the system are as described by Mrs. Hatch, but that they were paragons of moral purity. Let it be remembered that many of the persons described by Mr. H. are among the chief supporters of the system. A "new dispensation" which produces such fruits in the short space of ten or fifteen years must be regarded as satanic. But Mrs. Hatch continues:

"In the first place, spiritualists have generally the reputation of being impure, atheistical;

everything, in short, that is improper and unsafe. There is usually some ground for opinions so wide-spread. . . .

"With these facts before us, it is not surprising that many, after becoming acquainted with it, should have withdrawn from all recognition of it, and refused to countenance a system which is ignominy to those who have advocated it. . . . With sorrow we say it, many are the families which have been desolated by it. . . . Many thousands are the hearts and minds which have been broken and overthrown through this fatal delusion. . . . Further than this, we might dwell on the practices of professed spiritualists, but we have said enough."

These denunciations do not come from the opponents of Spiritualism, but from one of its warmest advocates. Mrs. Hatch has been behind the curtain, where she has seen a part of what has been hid from public gaze.

Not content with one lecture on the subject, she renews the attack, in the same place,

January 26th, 1862. On this occasion she says:

"The Church and Society are turned against Spiritualism. . . . because of the unholy, debasing effects to which it has been led. Cut where it may, the truth is that it is the character of too many of its prominent advocates which rendered Spiritualism unpopular. It has become a cloak for all debasing acts; a vehicle for all the dangerous theories that the brain of man, prompted by an evil spirit, has ever invented; we have become responsible for them all; and at last we are made to incite or justify every crime of the decalogue, and have become the confederates in every scheme of imposture which can lead to notoriety or gain. Thousands have been led to do what they knew to be wrong, because they have been assured that spirits desired it. . . . Broken-down physicians, briefless lawyers, placeless politicians, who have always been dependent upon their wives' relations or their own friends, go about the country as mediums, spiritual doctors, lecturers, etc., literally sponging their substance out of honest, hard-working people. Go to the smallest country town, and if you take interest enough to stay there a few days some person of this sort comes around, who seeks in some form to cause the people to believe that he is not the veriest impostor and scoundrel out of jail."

Here is a portrait of Spiritualism by one who is not supposed to represent it worse than it is. These "sweeping denunciations" of Mrs. Hatch do not seem to please Miss Emma Harding. Writing from New York to the "Banner of Light," March 1, 1862, she says:

"I believe we can none of us afford to condemn each other too loudly, lest we should be inviting a criticism we cannot endure." And yet she confesses that there are sufficient grounds for some of the charges. Perhaps the remark of Miss Harding, with regard to "inviting a criticism," etc., was intended as a thrust at Mrs.

Hatch, whom Spiritualism had led to violate her own marriage vow, and separate from the one to whom she promised before God to "keep herself" so long as they both should live. But Mrs. Hatch can no more reform the advocates of Spiritualism than she can convince a Christian community that the system is of God. It is simply the work of devils, and a stream does not rise above its fountain. "Wicked men and seducers wax worse and worse, deceiving and being deceived."

In conclusion, Spiritualism is attempting to popularize those social conditions of society, which are to be deeply deplored by every good citizen. "Iniquities which have justly received the condemnation of centuries are openly upheld; vices which would destroy every wholesome regulation of society are crowned as virtues;" and prostitution, the bane of domestic peace, is upheld and encouraged.

How timely is the wise man's counsel, "Regard not them that have familiar spirits, neither seek after wizards." "Let not thine heart incline to their ways; go not astray in their paths. Their house is the way to hell, going down to the chambers of death." "The dead are there and their guests are in the depths of hell." Prov. vii, 25–27; ix, 18.

THE END.

BOOKS FOR YOUNG PEOPLE.

200 Mulberry-street, New York.

PLEASANT PATHWAYS;

Or, Persuasives to Early Piety: containing Explanations and Illustrations of the Beauty, Safety, and Pleasantness of a Religious Life: being an Attempt to persuade Young People of both Sexes to seek Happiness in the Love and Service of Jesus Christ. By DANIEL WISE, author of "The Path of Life," "Young Man's Counselor," etc., etc. Two Illustrations. Wide 16mo.

The works of this author have secured him the reputation of one of the most eloquent and fascinating religious writers of the day. As a writer for youth we know of no one whom we should regard as his equal. The book before us will be found more fascinating than a novel; once commenced it will not be easy to lay it down.—*Christian Guardian.*

One of the most beautiful works, in our estimation, ever published. Its contents are as sands of gold—peculiarly adapted to impart precious thoughts which shall tend to noble aspirations for a Christian life.—*Buffalo Advocate.*

Well calculated to exert a salutary influence.—*Christian Intelligencer.*

Can scarcely be read without signal benefit, especially by the young.—*Pittsburgh Christian Advocate.*

Remarkable for depth of reasoning and tenderness. It must, by the blessing of God, win many to Christ. Praise God for such works.—*Beauty of Holiness.*

It does not clothe piety in weeds or hang salvation in black. It combines the good, the beautiful, and the true.—*Northwestern Christian Advocate.*

Will be read with lively interest by youth who are even uninterested in its purpose. The Christian parent can put it into the hands of his children with the assurance that it will prove a delight to them, while they cannot fail to learn its great lessons.—*Christian Advocate.*

Admirably adapted to do good.—*Vermont Christian Messenger.*

PALISSY THE POTTER;

Or, the Huguenot, Artist, and Martyr. A true Narrative. By C. L. BRIGHTWELL. Eighteen Illustrations. Wide 16mo.

Bernard de Palissy is the most perfect model of the workman. It is by his example, rather than by his works, that he has exercised an influence upon civilization, and that he has deserved a place to himself among the men who have ennobled humanity. Though he had remained unknown and listless, making tiles in his father's pottery; though he had never purified, molded, or enameled his handful of clay; though his living groups, his crawling reptiles, his slimy snails, his slippery frogs, his lively lizards, and his damp herbs and dripping mosses had never adorned those dishes, ewers, and salt-cellars—those quaint and elaborate ornaments of the tables and cupboards of the sixteenth century; it is true nothing would have been wanting to the art of Phidias or of Michael Angelo—to the porcelain of Sèvres, of China, of Florence, or Japan; but we should not have had his life for the operative to admire and imitate.—*Lamartine.*

THE RAINBOW SIDE:

A Sequel to "The Itinerant." By Mrs. C. M. EDWARDS. Four Illustrations. Wide 16mo.

The Young Lady's Counselor;

Or, Outlines and Illustrations of the Sphere, the Duties, and the Dangers of Young Women. By Rev. D. WISE. 12mo.

The Young Man's Counselor;

Or, Sketches and Illustrations of the Duties and Dangers of Young Men. Designed to be a Guide to Success in this Life, and to Happiness in the Life which is to come. By Rev. D. WISE, 12mo.

The Path of Life;

Or, Sketches of the Way to Glory and Immortality. A Help to Young Christians. By Rev. DANIEL WISE. 16mo.

The object of this book, to "help young Christians," is truly great a[illegible] noble. The author, we think, has carried out his design with signal ability. Mr. Wise writes with great clearness, and is always both attractive and instructive.

Bridal Greetings,

With Marriage Certificate. By Rev. D. WISE. 24mo.

This work is intended for a gift book to the newly married. It is eminently practical in its hints, and being cheap, is just the thing for ministers to present to parties whose marriage they are employed to solemnize.

Guide to the Saviour;

Or, the Lambs of the Flock of Jesus. By Rev. D. WISE

Just the thing for little children.

The Swiss Reformer;

Or, the Life of Ulric Zwingle. By Rev. DANIEL WISE.

Wanderer, Come Home; [In preparation.]

Or, the Good Shepherd seeking his Lost Sheep: being an affectionate Call to Backsliders. By Rev. D. WISE.

Moral and Religious Quotations

From the Poets. Topically Arranged. Comprising choice Selections from six hundred Authors. Compiled by Rev. WILLIAM RICE, A.M. 8vo.

We have seen many dictionaries of quotations, but this surpasses them all in extent and system. The subjects are those that come before the preacher's mind, and he will open this book as he is preparing a sermon, and find happy lines to adorn and enrich his discourse, and astonish his hearers by his familiarity with the poets! It will also lead him to the study of poetry, and introduce him to authors whose acquaintance he would never have cultivated, but for these brief and sententious extracts from their works. More than four thousand quotations are here made.—*New York Observer.*

Pronouncing Bible.

Large 8vo.

We have lately issued the best Bible in print, a PRONOUNCING BIBLE, having these advantages: 1. The proper names are divided and accented, so that a child can pronounce them correctly. 2. Each book has a short introduction, showing just what every reader ought to know about it. 3. It has a much improved class of references. 4. It contains a map of Old Canaan and its surroundings, and one of Palestine, according to the latest discoveries.

The method is more simple and easy than any other we have seen. The pronunciation marks are very judiciously confined to the proper names, leaving the remainder of the text unencumbered. The multitudes of Bible readers who stumble at the hard names of people and places may find a very satisfactory relief by using this edition. For family worship, or private devotional reading, this edition has strong recommendations.—*Presbyterian.*

In this Bible the proper names are divided into syllables and accented, so that it is hardly possible to mispronounce them. The "Introductions" are brief, but contain a large amount of useful and necessary information. The "references," as far as we have had time to test them, are decidedly the most accurate we have met with. It is one of the most beautiful and complete Bibles in the world, and it will be an acquisition to the study, the family, the Bible class and the pulpit.—*Evangelical Witness.*

Rudiments of Public Speaking

And Debate; Or, Hints on the Application of Logic. By J. G. Holyoake, author of "Mathematics no Mystery," "Logic of Facts," etc. With an Essay on Sacred Eloquence by Henry Rogers. Revised, with Notes, by Rev. L. D. Barrows. 12mo.

"Speech is the body, thought the soul, and suitable action the lips of eloquence." He has oratory who ravishes his hearers, while he forgets himself.—*Lavater.* Eloquence is vehement simplicity.—*Cecil.*

The object of this book is to assist public speakers in perfecting themselves in the art of speaking effectively. Too many exhaust themselves on the *matter* f their discourse, and utterly fail in the *manner* of it. The tendency of this oook is to correct this error, and secure a better and more impressive style. Please read the following notices of it:

We cordially commend Dr. Barrows's volume to all ministers, young and old, and in fact to public speakers of all classes. It is full of marrow and fatness.—*Western Advocate.*

A close study of it will save the young public speaker from many blunders which, if uncorrected, will impair his usefulness and hinder his success.—*Northern Advocate.*

Our preachers will do well to send for it. A clergyman of great intellectual power, though being favored with little success, when asked how much of a sermon was due to the manner in which it was delivered, answered "Three fourths."—*Ch istian Advocate and Journal.*

There is nothing dry or dull in the entire book. It is full of most valuable suggestions, so presented as to be remembered.—*Congregational Herald.*

The Christian Maiden.

Memorials of Eliza Hessel. By Joshua Priestley. Slightly abridged from the second London edition. With a Portrait and Vignette. 12mo.

Much of the religious biography of the day is both commonplace and insipid. There are, however, many choice exceptions, and among such we class the interesting memoir before us. Miss Hessel was a young lady who cultivated her mind to the utmost, and diffused a cheering influence in the circle in which she moved. Her biography is replete with illustrations of the deep Christian experience, and varied and extensive reading. We cordially commend this little book to Christian young women, as well calculated to impr ve the understanding and purify the heart.—*Ch istian Guardian.*

Quotations from the Poets.

Moral and Religious Quotations from the Poets. Com piled by Rev. WILLIAM RICE, A. M. Large octavo, with frontispiece.

Half calf, marbled edges, with two plates

Royal octavo edition, nine steel plates.

Morocco, gilt.......
———, *extra gilt*

New Pronouncing Bible.

Royal octavo. The proper names are accented and divided, so that the most common reader can pronounce them.

Morocco, with maps, plates, and gilt edges
———, *extra*
In 4 vols., imitation morocco, marbled edges
The same, gilt edges

Hidden Treasure.

Four Illustrations. Wide 16mo.

Story of a Pocket Bible.

Ten Illustrations. Wide 16mo.

Ministering Children.

A Story showing how even a Child may be as a Ministering Angel of Love to the Poor and Sorrowful. Fifteen Illustrations. Wide 16mo.

gilt edges
Morocco and full calf

Whedon's Commentary.

A Commentary of the Gospels of Matthew and Mark. Intended for Popular Use. By D. D. WHEDON, D.D. 12mo.

The first volume of this work has been on sale for the past year and a large number of volumes have been sold. It is a 12mo. of 422 closely printed pages, embracing a fine map of Palestine, and other valuable illustrations. It is the cheapest book for the price that we have issued in many years. The two volumes which are to follow will be announced in due time. All the notices we have seen, as well as the remarks we have heard, go to the effect that this book is a timely, able, and valuable addition to our literature.

Dr. Whedon has furnished the people with the results of critical study, modern travels and Christian reflection, in brief and pithy comments on the difficult or obscure words and phrases in the first two evangelists, enlarging on occasional passages of importance.—*Congregational Herald.*

It gives the results of patient study and the careful examination of the works of those who have preceded him in the same field, in few words well chosen.—*Christ. Observer, Phila.*

Dr. Whedon is one of the clearest, strongest, and boldest writers in America. He addresses the intellect, not the passions; reason, not the feelings. The principal value of this commentary is found in exposition, while its real spiritual utility will depend much on the piety of the reader, and hence a boundless field is before him. Religious truths are presented in vivid distinctness; the popular mind is instructed.—*Richmond Christ. Adv.*

The Pioneer Bishop;

Or, the Life and Times of FRANCIS ASBURY. By W. P. STRICKLAND, D.D. 12mo.

One of the most fascinating volumes of biography ever issued from our press.—*Quarterly Review.*

This is at once a charming volume and a marvelous record.—*New York Commercial Advertiser.*

This book will be read, and will exert a beneficial influence wherever read.—*Zion's Herald.*

The author has performed his duty well, and with a catholicity of spirit worthy of honor.—*New York Intelligencer.*

No one can have a just view of the rise and settlement of the Methodist Episcopal Church in the United States without carefully perusing this book. —*Dr. Durbin.*

PUBLISHED BY CARLTON & PORTER,

200 Mulberry-street, New York.

Little Songs for Little Readers.

With numerous Illustrations. Wide 16mo.

This book of songs is just what the little folks in our Sunday schools and families have long wanted.

Ministry of Life.

Five Illustrations. Wide 16mo.

gilt

Morocco and full calf, gilt

The Christian Maiden.

Memorials of Miss Eliza Hessel. Wide 16mo.

Muslin, gilt edges

Morocco, gilt edges

A perfect gem.

My Sister Margaret.

Four Illustrations. Wide 16mo.

gilt

Morocco and full calf

The best temperance book in print.

Pilgrim's Progress.

With numerous Illustrations. 12mo.

imitation morocco, gilt

The Object of Life.

A Narrative Illustrating the Insufficiency of the World and the Sufficiency of Christ. With four Illustrations. Wide 16mo.

full calf, gilt

PUBLISHED BY CARLTON & PORTER,

200 Mulberry-street, New York.

A Pretty Little Library.

Ten Volumes. 48mo.

WILBUR'S TRIP TO THE SEA-SHORE.
THE BLACKBERRY GIRL.
MY LITTLE SCHOOLMATES.
BESSIE'S THREE TEACHERS.
BESSIE'S NEW HEART.
LITTLE STORIES FOR LITTLE PEOPLE.
MY GRANDMOTHER.
MY BEST FRIEND.
THE LITTLE PARTNERS, ETC.
ENGLISH MARY.

The Jessie Books.

Five Volumes. 18mo.

JESSIE ROSS.
JESSIE SAYS SO.
JESSIE'S GOLDEN RULE.
JESSIE'S PLACE.
JESSIE A PILGRIM.

The JESSIE BOOKS are full of interest. No better Christmas or New-years present for boys or girls under thirteen—girls especially—will issue from the press this season than this box of Jessie Books.

Child's Own Library, No. 1.

Twenty Volumes.

Child's Own Library, No. 2.

Twenty Volumes.

BOOKS FOR SUNDAY SCHOOLS.

200 Mulberry-street New York.

THE YOUNG MINER:

A Memoir of John Lean, Jun., of Camborne, in the County of Cornwall. By JOHN BUSTARD. 18mo.

THANET SUNDAY-SCHOOL TEACHER.

Mildred, the Thanet S. School Teacher. By JOHN BUSTARD. 18mo.

OLD HUMPHREY'S OBSERVATIONS.

Selections from Old Humphrey's Observations and Addresses. Six Illustrations. 18mo.

INTERESTING STORIES

For the Entertainment and Instruction of Young Readers. Illustrated. Two volumes, 18mo.

ELLEN AND SOPHIA;

Or, The Broken Hyacinth. By MRS. SHERWOOD, Author of "Little Henry and his Bearer." Three Illustrations. 18mo.

FARMER GOODALL AND HIS FRIEND.

By the Author of "The Last Day of the Week." With Illustrations. 18mo.

JANE AND HER TEACHER.

A Simple Story. 18mo.

THE MOUNTAIN AND VALLEY.

Two Illustrations. 18mo.

PROCRASTINATION;

Or, Maria Louisa Winslow. By MRS. H. M. PICKARD. 18mo.

CHRISTIAN PEACE;

Or, The Third Fruit of the Spirit. Illustrated by Scenes from Real Life. 18mo.

THE CAVES OF THE EARTH:

Their Natural History, Features, and Incidents. 18mo.

THE BLIND MAN'S SON;

Or, The Poor Student successfully struggling to overcome Adversity and Misfortune. Two Illustrations. 18mo.

BOOKS FOR YOUNG PEOPLE.

200 Mulberry-street, New York.

THE POET PREACHER:

A Brief Memorial of Charles Wesley, the eminent Preacher and Poet. By CHARLES ADAMS. Five Illustrations. Wide 16mo.

WORDS THAT SHOOK THE WORLD;

Or, Martin Luther his own Biographer. Being Pictures of the Great Reformer, sketched mainly from his own Sayings. By CHARLES ADAMS. Twenty-two Illustrations. Wide 16mo

MINISTERING CHILDREN:

A Story showing how even a Child may be as a Ministering Angel of Love to the Poor and Sorrowful. Wide 16mo Illustrated

This is one of the most moving narrations in the whole list of our publications. Its sale in England has reached 40,000 copies. The illustrated edition contains more than a dozen superb cuts on plate paper.

THE MINISTRY OF LIFE.

By MARIA LOUISA CHARLESWORTH, Author of "Ministering Children," etc., etc. Five Illustrations. Wide 16mo.

ITINERANT SIDE;

Or, Pictures of Life in the Itinerancy. Illustrated. Wide 16mo.

THE OBJECT OF LIFE:

A Narrative illustrating the Insufficiency of the World, and the Sufficiency of Christ. Four Illustration. Wide 16mo.

LADY HUNTINGDON PORTRAYED;

Including Brief Sketches of some of her Friends and Co-laborers. By the Author of "The Missionary Teacher," "Sketches of Mission Life," etc. Five Illustrations.

THE MOTHER'S MISSION.

Sketches from Real Life. By the Author of "The Object of Life." Five Illustrations. Wide 16mo.

MY SISTER MARGARET.

A Temperance Story. By Mrs. C. M. EDWARDS. Four Illustrations. Wide 16mo

www.ingramcontent.com/pod-product-compliance
Lightning Source LLC
LaVergne TN
LVHW050530100826
845148LV00002B/511

* 9 7 8 1 4 2 5 5 1 9 0 8 7 *